Carving a Street-Corner Band

Al Streetman

Foreword by Sylvester Tillman

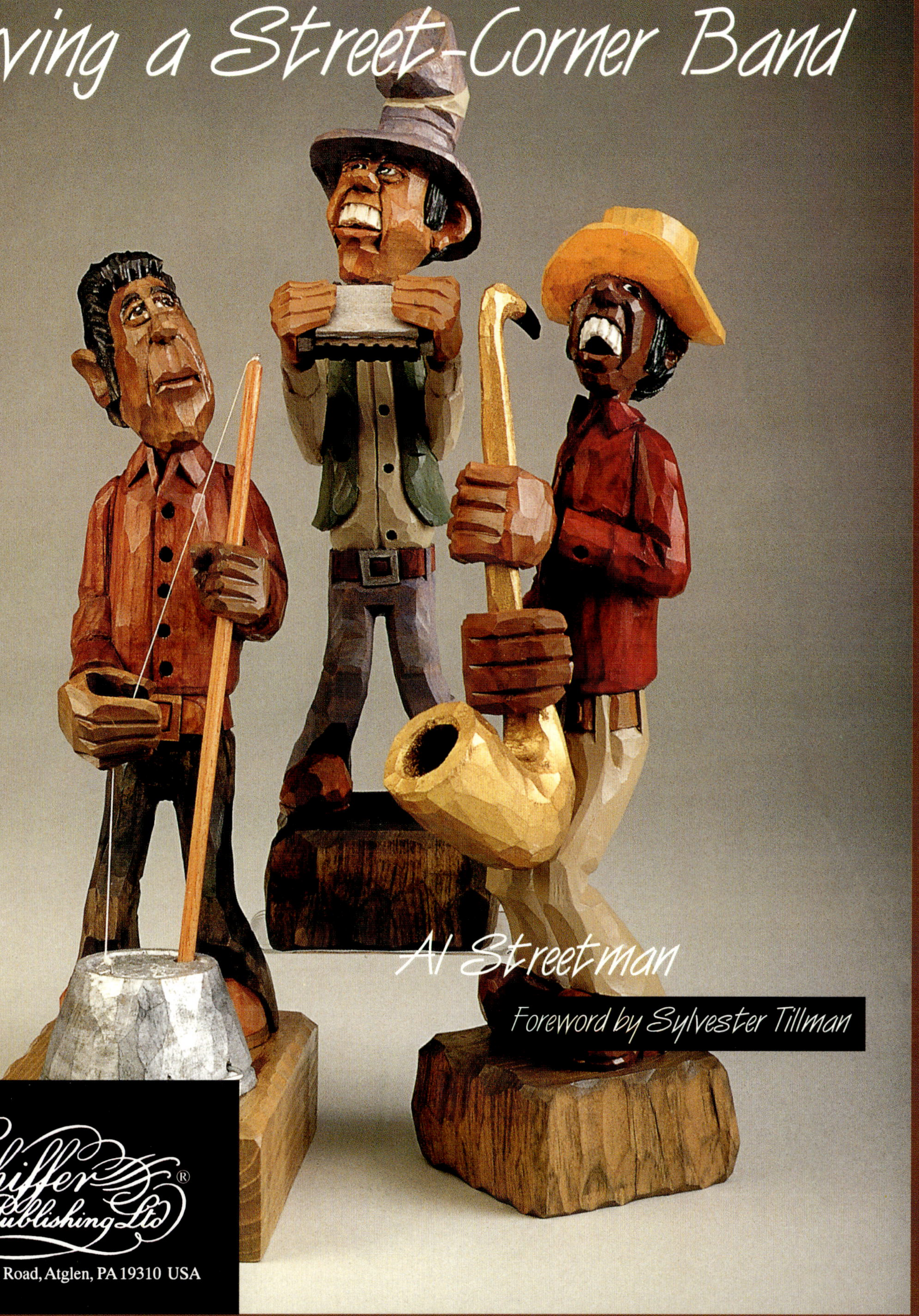

Schiffer Publishing Ltd®
4880 Lower Valley Road, Atglen, PA 19310 USA

Acknowledgments

The following people helped make this book possible. I thank you all.

Gary and Scott Voorhies:Woodcrafters of Oklahoma; High-quality carving tools and supplies.
Tim and Deborah Effrem: WoodCarvers Supply, Inc.; Excellent assortment of fine carving tools, supplies, and books.
Peter Gill: Robert Sorby fine tools; Excellent gouges and knives.
David Mather: Tuckaway Timber Company, LLC.; High-quality Basswood, White Pine, Butternut and Tupelo for carving.
DecoArt: The paint samples were excellent, and satisfactory in all respects.
Royal Brush Mfg.,Inc.: Excellent quality paintbrushes at an affordable price.

If you have trouble finding any of the supplies discussed in this book, please feel free to contact me for a list of carving sources and suppliers:

Al Streetman
402 North Broad Street
Guthrie, Oklahoma, 73044
E-mail: astreetman@mmcable.com

Library of Congress Card Number: 00-111686

Designed by John P. Cheek
Type set in Van Dijk/Souvenir Lt BT
ISBN: 0-7643-1328-2
Printed in China

Published by Schiffer Publishing Ltd.
4880 Lower Valley Road
Atglen, PA 19310
Phone: (610) 593-1777; Fax: (610) 593-2002
E-mail: Schifferbk@aol.com
Please visit our web site catalog at
www.schifferbooks.com or write for a free catalog.

In Europe, Schiffer books are distributed by
Bushwood Books
6 Marksbury Ave.
Kew Gardens
Surrey TW9 4JF England
Phone: 44 (0)20-8392-8585; Fax: 44 (0)20-8392-9876
E-mail: Bushwd@aol.com
Free postage in the UK. Europe: Air mail at cost.
Please try your bookstore first.

Contents

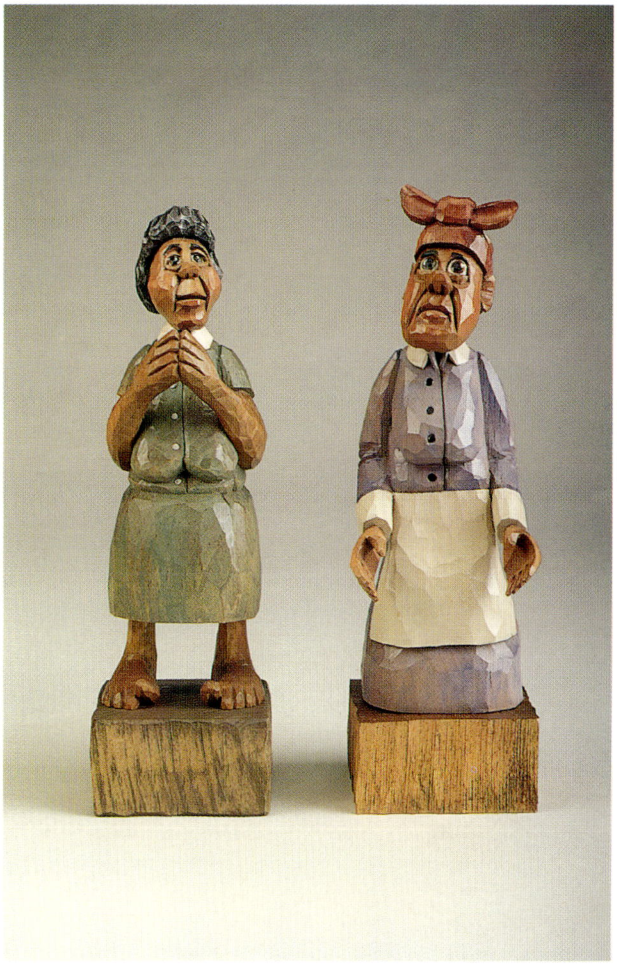

Foreword

Hello,

My name is Sylvester Tillman. I am an African-American from Natchez, Mississippi. I have known Al Streetman for at least 10 years, and we have become really good friends in the last 5 or 6 years. I have always admired Al's carvings in wood, because they are so unique and humorous. I remember Al's first Santa book. When I saw it, I laughed the whole way through, and I thought "Here is a man who carves because he enjoys it; he is having fun". For the last couple of years, I have asked him to do some more of his magic, but to do some caricatures in Black. What Al has come up with in this book is such great stuff, I'm thinking about picking up a knife myself.

Al is a man of moral character and humility, and he was worried about the way some people might take his vision as not being politically correct. Al asked me to look at and review all the patterns in this book, and make sure I did not find anything offensive or stereotypical about them. Again, Al's work is art with a neat sense of humor. His carvings appeal to all of humankind. I am honored that he chose me to write this foreword, and that he is using my name in the street corner band. I say "Hurray for Al, and good job!...I like it. You can carve Black cowboys the next time. They are hard to find, even in Oklahoma. For the people who are upset at these carvings, I say "get a life—there is nothing bad here". I have seen Al do cowboys, Santas, fishermen, gnomes, and other things, and they have always brought a smile to my face. I plan on buying the street corner band myself and displaying it in my living room. Folks, look, do not get carried away about the wrong things here....it's art, and nothing more. If the book gives you warm fuzzies buy it, use it, enjoy it. I know I will.

(Signed),

Sylvester Tillman

Sylvester (Junior) Tillman

Introduction

Over the years, I have had numerous requests from Black carvers and Black collectors, asking me to do a book which features Black people as the primary focus. After taking a hard look, I realized that, indeed, there were hardly any patterns which lent themselves to being wrought as a Black person. I made a promise that if I could develop some patterns which did not portray a stereotypical image of Black Americans, I would move forward in developing a book.

Pushing me from the home front was a good friend of mine, Sylvester (Junior) Tillman,(who incidentally is Black), urging me year after year to do a book which featured Black characters. We kicked a few ideas around, and the street-corner band was born.

I let Sly scrutinize every pattern in the book, and he approved of them all. After having done many books featuring Santa, Cowboys, Leprechauns and other caricatures, this book was a refreshing change of pace. There are still lots of Santa books and others on my idea board, but for now, let's concentrate of getting this project carved. The sooner you get him done, the sooner you can have the rest of the band completed. Then you can stay awake at night yelling at them to hold down the music, and I can finally get some sleep!

We will go through one project in full detail, from carving to painting, to finishing. The other patterns are similar, so once you go through the project, the techniques presented can be applied to them, in order to complete the band and onlookers.

Some of you may observe that my carving project is not as complex or detailed as you might carve it. *There is a method to my madness.* In this book, as in my previous books, I have tried to design a project that would yield a nice result, yet not be so complex or involved that the beginning wood carver would not be able to accomplish it. I want to reach as many wood carvers as possible, and share the joy of carving with them. As the beginners gain more experience, they can add additional details as desired.

Except for the actual carving project, I have not included specific carving instructions. I have found that each carver has his or her own style, and each has their preference for which tool to use in a particular area, or to achieve a particular effect.

Rather than giving a vague instruction such as "use a small gouge", I have listed the particular size tool I used in the different steps of the carving project, as we move through each step of the carving. This is more for the benefit of the beginning carver, rather than the more experienced ones. If you don't have these particular sizes of gouges or tools, use something similar.

Each pattern in this book shows all the component pieces needed to make that particular carving. All the pieces are in scale to each other, so if you enlarge or reduce a pattern, the pattern pieces will still be in the right proportion to each other. Should you desire a larger or smaller version, simply enlarge or shrink the pattern on a photocopying machine (in the "Tips" section, I explain reducing and enlarging patterns with a copying machine if this is new to you).

On the patterns, you will notice an arrow with a "G" superimposed over it. This arrow indicates the recommended grain direction of the wood in relation to the pattern, in order to make carving that particular piece as easy as possible.

I use Basswood whenever possible, but any soft wood such as Jelutong, clear Spruce, or Sugar/White Pine will work equally well. Try to obtain wood that is relatively knot and burl free. Nothing is more frustrating than trying to work a pattern around a big, old knot! If possible, use a bandsaw with a 1/8" or 3/16" blade to cut out the pattern pieces. The bandsaw will allow you to release the rough version of the pattern from the block of wood faster than trying to use a coping saw or other means to cut out the pattern.

General Notes

1. Trace the pattern pieces, or make a copy of them on a photocopying machine. Glue the pattern you copied or traced onto some heavy paper such as poster paper or a manila file folder. When the glue is dry, cut out the pattern. This method will prevent you from ruining the master patterns in your book.
2. Lay your pattern on the wood, trace the outline of it, and saw it out. *Pay close attention to any recommended grain directions indicated on the pattern pieces!*
3. You should now have a rough blank ready to be carved.
4. Use your own techniques and style to bring the carving to the finished stage.
5. In the "Tips" section, there is information describing hand carving separately from the arm, if you are not familiar with this technique.
6. *I recommend that you read the entire book before starting the project.* This will help you see where we are going, and will help alert you to carving techniques that may be unfamiliar. In the section where we paint the project, you may see an area or detail that might not have been clear to you in the carving section. Reading the entire book through before beginning the project will help you identify any such areas, and may help eliminate frustration at a later time. Remember, if we carve it, we will paint it, so you will see everything at least twice.
7. If you see a pattern that you wish to carve, *pay close attention to the pattern page*. Although I submit all the patterns to the publisher full-size, it may be necessary for a certain number of them to be reduced in size in order to meet the page requirements of the book. If a particular pattern has been reduced in size, it will be so indicated somewhere on the pattern. The information I included in the "Tips" section concerning enlarging/reducing will tell you how to get the pattern back to full-size, or any other size you may wish to make it.

Project Carving Tools

I have been using gouges made by Robert Sorby. They are reasonably priced and have great edge-holding ability. Listed here are the gouges I used to create this project:

1/8" "V" gouge
1/4" "V" gouge
1/4" straight gouge
1/2" straight gouge
3mm"U" gouge
5mm "U" gouge
10mm "U" gouge

For those of you who are not familiar with the type of cuts different gouges make, or how large the cut is for a specific size of gouge, I have included a Gouge Reference Chart in this book. If you want to use a different gouge other than one which I used, this chart will be helpful in determining what type of gouge you might want to try.

Gouge Reference Chart

General Woodcarving Gouges

	Inch	mm
Square Chisel		
	3/8	10
Skew Chisels		
	1/8	3
	3/8	10
Straight Gouges		
	1/4	6
	1/2	13
	3/4	19
	1/8	3
	1/4	6
	3/8	10
	1/2	13
	3/16	5
	3/8	10
	1/8	3
	3/8	10
	3/4	19
Veiners		
	1/8	3
	1/16	1.5
	1/4	6
Bent Gouges		
	3/4	19
	3/8	10
Spoon Bit Gouges		
	3/8	10
	3/8	10
V Tools		
	1/8	3
	1/4	6

Micro Carving Gouges

	Blade Size
Square Chisel	5mm
Skew Chisel	4mm
Dog Leg Chisel	5mm
Straight Gouges	2mm
	3mm
	4mm
	5mm
	5mm
Bent Gouges	3mm
	5mm
Veiner	2.5mm
V Parting Tool	3mm

Reprinted with the permission of Robert Sorby

Carving Tips

1. Here are some different ways to carve eyes:

A. **Quilt pin method:** I often use various sizes of plastic-head quilting pins to make eyes. Mark where you want the eyes to be on the finished carving. Using a drill and bit that is slightly larger than the pin head you are going to use, make a hole for each eye. Using wire cutters, snip off the pin head, leaving about 1/4" of the pin attached to the head. Insert the pin head into the eye socket, with the pin end going in first. Use a nail set to seat the head into the hole until only a small orb protrudes. This gives a fairly realistic eye without causing too much effort on your part. For extra detail, remove a triangular-shaped piece of wood from the sides of the pin head. This will make a very realistic eye when it is painted.

B. **Punch method:** A second way to create eyes the easy way is to use carver's eye punches. Select the size eye punch you want to use, based on the size of the eye sockets you have made. Push the eye punch against the socket firmly and rotate it. After making both eyes, remove triangular-shaped pieces of wood from the corners to give more detail. Use your knife, if necessary, to smooth and round off the eyeball.

C. **Football method:** A more realistic way to make eyes is to first of all carve the eye sockets so that about a 90° angle is formed. Lightly sketch in a football-shaped eye in each socket, such that the top half of the football is on the upper half of the socket, and the lower half of the football is on the lower half of the socket. When you sketch in the footballs, make the outside ends lower than the inside ends. Using the tip of your knife, score the football outline to a depth of about 1/16". Now use the tip of your knife to remove triangular-shaped pieces of wood from the left and right corner of each eye. This will leave a small section of wood inside each football, which will be the eyeball. use your knife to round off and smooth the eyeball. You can vary the way you remove the triangular-shaped corners, if you want the eyes to be looking more to one side, rather than straight ahead.

D. **Mound method:** The most realistic way to make eyes is to first rough-carve the nose so it is standing out from the face. Next, sketch a circle or oval on each side of the nose to represent where the eye mounds will be located. Using a smaller "V" gouge such as a 1/8" size, or your knife tip, go around the circles or ovals so the mounds will be defined, and separated from the face area. Use your knife to round the sharp edges of the mounds, and the face area around the mounds.

Divide the mounds into thirds by sketching two curved horizontal lines across each one, making sure that the lines join at each corner of the mound (look at your own eyes in a mirror to see what I mean here). Using your knife tip, score each horizontal line about 1/16" deep. Working from the *center* of the eye mound, use your knife tip to shave *upward* toward the top horizontal line, and *downward* toward the bottom horizontal line. This will make the eyelids stand out from the eyeball area. Finally, remove small triangular pieces of wood from each corner of the eye, so the eyeball will be rounded from left to right, as well as top to bottom.

Changing the size and shape of the mounds, and the spacing between the horizontal lines, will allow you to achieve many effects and expressions on your carvings.

One last thing concerning eyes: Don't get upset if you discover that you have carved one eye smaller or at a different angle than the other eye. This "accident" may work to your advantage. It will lend an interesting variation to the carving, and no one has to know you didn't do it that way on purpose!

2. When buying wood, whether it be Basswood, White pine, Spruce, or some other type, try to pick the *lightest* pieces. They tend to have less fat and sap in them, so they are easier to carve. I have been obtaining my carving wood from Tuckaway Timber. Their address is listed in the Sources of Supplies included in this book.

3. An easy way to help determine where you want to place some wrinkles and folds in the arms, torso, and legs is to observe and note where the wood grain changes direction as you are carving. Usually in the crook of an elbow or behind the knees, you will notice that wood "fuzzies" try to appear, no matter how carefully you carve or how sharp your knife is. That is because the wood grain direction is changing, and in one direction or the other, you are trying to carve against the grain, thus the "fuzzies" appear. These spots are perfect candidates for wrinkles and folds, made with a large "V" tool or by cutting wedges out with your knife. As a beginning carver, if you do nothing more than add a few cuts in these areas, you will be amazed at the difference in the way the carving looks. With experience, you will start noticing other places to add wrinkles and folds.

4. For those of you who have never had much practice enlarging or reducing patterns, or being able to calculate how much enlargement or reduction you need to select on the photocopying machine, here are some general guidelines:

Let's say you have a pattern that shows a side profile requiring 2" thick wood, and you want to make the pattern larger so it will fit on 3" thick wood. Use the following formula to calculate what percentage enlargement to select on the copier:

[New Dimension Desired ÷ Present Dimension] x 100 = %

Using our example, this would work out as follows:

[3" ÷ 2"] x100 = **150 %**

Going the other way, let's say you have a pattern that shows a 2" side profile, and you want to reduce it down so it will fit on a piece of 1 3/4" thick wood. Using the same formula, it works out as follows:

[1.75" ÷ 2"] x 100 = **87.5 %**

If the machine you are using won't go large enough or small enough to get the job done on the first try, additional steps may be required. Go ahead and make your first copy using the largest enlargement or reduction setting you can select. Measure the *new* dimensions on your *copy* (which will now be your Present Dimension), then use the same formula as before to calculate how much additional enlargement or reduction is needed to get the pattern to the size you desire it to be.

5. When making separate hands that are going to be holding some object, it is easiest if you first cut out the top profile of the hand, drill a hole large enough for the object to fit through, then saw out the side profile of the hand. This procedure will help prevent the hand from splitting when you drill it.

6. For those patterns where the hands are to be carved separately, the following instructions may be used if you are not familiar with this method of hand carving:

A. Lay out the top view of the hands on a piece of 3/4" thick basswood. Leave a short section of wood at the rear of each hand when you lay out the pattern. This section will serve as a handle while you carve and shape the hands, and will form the wrist pegs in a later step. Saw out the top profile of the hands.

B. Now, using the top set of hands in the Hand Studies as a reference, sketch in the side profile of the hands, then saw them out. You now should have two hands that will require very little work to finish.

C. Sketch in the thumbs. Remove wood from each hand using a knife or a **#7 10mm "U" gouge**, so the thumbs are well-defined, then round off the sharp edges of the thumbs.

D. Draw a line in the middle of the finger section to divide it in half. Now draw lines to divide each of these sections in half. You should now have four fingers defined, all approximately equal.

E. Using a **1/8" "V" gouge**, go over these lines so the fingers will be separated. As an option, to add further detail without too much pain on your part, use a bandsaw, scroll saw or coping saw to carefully saw along these lines. Use your knife to remove any fuzzy wood caused by the saw cuts, and to remove any sharp edges still remaining on the hands. At this point, if you do nothing else, you will have two hands that will look perfectly good once they are painted. Experienced carvers may add more detailing as they desire, such as knuckles and wrinkles on the finger joints.

F. Using your knife, trim down the sections of wood protruding from the rear of the hands, so as to form a "wrist" or "pin" that will fit snugly into the holes you drilled earlier in the arms. When done properly, the hand should appear to be coming out of the sleeve. This method allows you to turn the hands in various directions, so your carvings will appear more lifelike.

General Painting Suggestions & Paintbrush Recommendations

I have included some *suggested* colors and paint brushes for all patterns. If you have a preference for a different color scheme, by all means use it. After all, it's your carving, and you can paint it any way you desire.

I have also listed the colors produced by DecoArt and their identification numbers, which I have found to be suitable for painting these carvings. I have used these colors, and the results were excellent. I hope this will help minimize your confusion when trying to sort through the maze of paint brands and colors at your hobby or craft store.

The best paintbrushes I have found, for the money, are made by the Royal Brush Mfg. Company. They come in a wide assortment of sizes and shapes, are durable, and most important are affordable. In general, here are the ones I use and recommend for painting your carvings.

Royal Golden Taklon series 250 Round, size 0 and 00: Details such as eyes and other small areas.

Royal Golden Taklon series 170 Cat's Tongue, size 2 and 4: Large areas.

Royal Golden Taklon series 150 Short Shader, size 2 and 4: Blending colors. (For example, when blending a "blush" color into the flesh color on faces, hands, etc.)

You may have heard and read this a million times, but when painting your carvings, keep the word *thin* in mind. What you want to do is stain the wood to give it some color and life, but you don't want the paint so thick that it covers up the beauty of the wood. **Note:** When painting faces and hair, I generally use a little thicker mixture of paint than I use on the rest of the carving. I want the face to be a bit more intense than the rest of the carving, since the head and face is what sets most of the mood for the carving.

Suggested Colors

Colors for the carving project:

Titanium White DA1
DeLane's Cheek Color DA182
Khaki Tan DA173
Calico Red DA20
Raw Sienna DA93
Royal Gold DM03
Lamp Black DA67
Walnut Gel Stain DS29
Marigold DA194
Light Cinnamon DA114
Burnt Sienna DA63
Brilliant Silver DM04
Satin Varnish DS21

Additional colors you may want to use for the other characters in the book:

Blush Flesh DA110
Shimmering Silver DA70
Dried Basil Green DA198
Pink Chiffon DA192
Camel DA191
Reindeer Moss Green DA187
Arbor Green DA209
Rookwood Red DA97
Dark Chocolate DA65
Honey Brown DA163
French Vanilla DA184
Petal Pink DA 214
Deep Periwinkle DA212
Payne's Grey DA167
Eggshell DA153
Pineapple DA6
Burnt Umber DA64

If you cannot find these colors locally, you can contact DecoArt at: **http://www.decoart.com.** They will be glad to tell you where a dealer is located close to you, and in many cases will provide you with samples of some of the colors for you to try.

Remember, these are only a few of the many colors you can use for your carvings. Should you have other color preferences, use them. Don't be afraid to get wild and experiment with all sorts of color combinations. For those of you (like me), who have difficulty trying to decide which colors work well together, most hobby and art supply stores sell inexpensive color wheels which will show you colors that work together, and colors that oppose each other. I have listed a few combinations here, for illustrative purposes:

Main Color	Contrast Color
Red	Green
Orange	Blue
Yellow	Violet

A good color wheel will not only show you main and contrast colors, it will also show colors that blend.

"Antiquing" the Project

Once the paint is dry, you may want to "age" your carving with an antiquing product in order to help tone down the colors a bit. I have had excellent results using antiquing gels made by DecoArt. These are available at hobby and craft stores. They come in various colors, so you can create different effects.

Brush a coat of antiquing gel on the wood, then wipe it off using a damp rag or sponge. It is your option how much you wipe off. After the antiquing is dry, I like to finish my carvings with a coat of brush-on acrylic varnish. DecoArt also makes an excellent varnish. I prefer the one that leaves a satin finish. This particular finish is not too flat nor too glossy, but leaves a "soft" look to the completed carving (I usually put a coat of varnish on the face, hands and other flesh areas *before* I antique the carving). This will prevent these areas from absorbing too much antiquing color.

Carving the Project

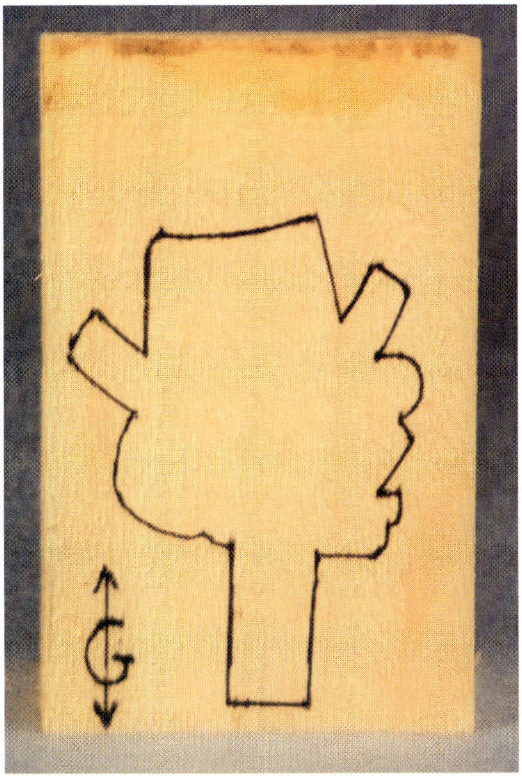

Transfer the side view of the head to a piece of wood of the appropriate thickness and width. I am using a 3" x 3" block of white pine, which we will adjust for the proper width in the next step. Saw out the side profile using a band saw, or other means available to you.

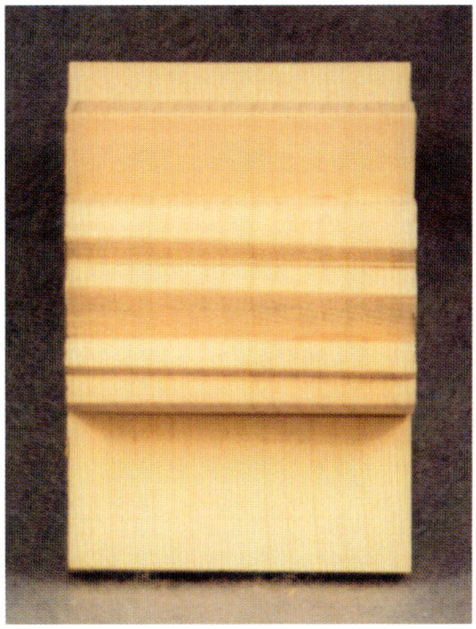

Here is a front view of the head, sawn to the proper width. I have left the neck a little long for now. We'll adjust the length in a later step, when we fit the head to the body.

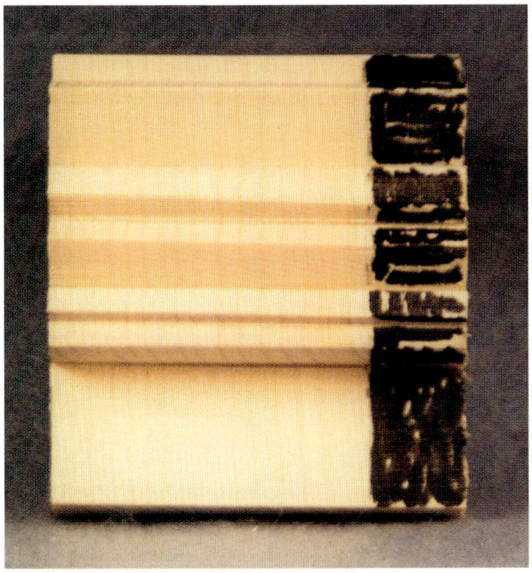

As a rule of thumb, if I am carving a character who is wearing a hat, I measure the length of the brim from front to back on the side view. This is the dimension I use to set the width of the head. Doing it this way provides a fairly square head block to start with, and will result in a fairly round brim when the hat is rounded off. On my pattern, I measured about 2 3/8" from front to back, so that is the width I have marked off here. I will saw away the darkened section, since it has now been declared "waste" wood.

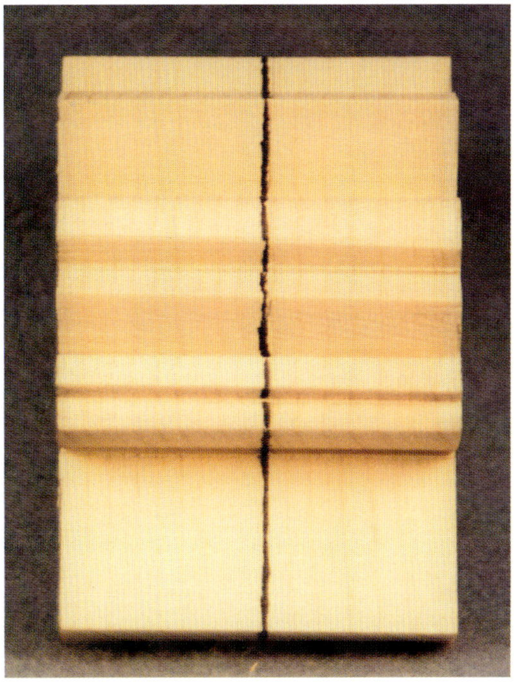

To help maintain symmetry as we carve the head, sketch a center line down the front of the head...

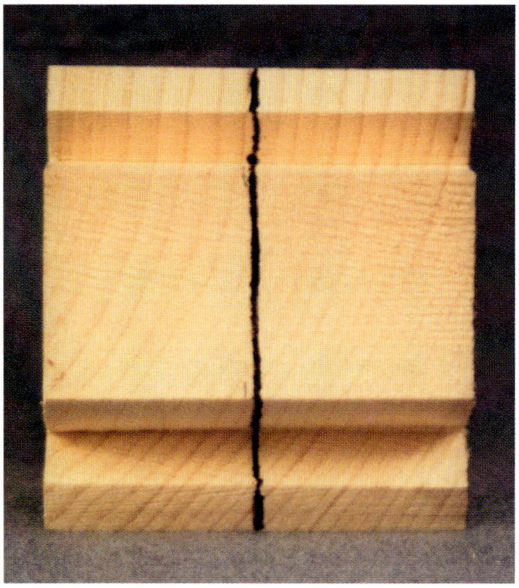

Over the crown of the hat.....

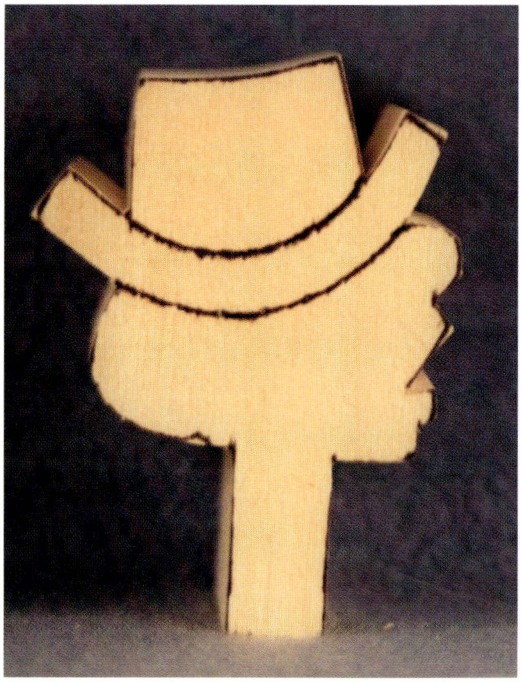

Sketch in the brim on one side of the head. **Tip:** Lay the pattern in place against the head, and prick the outline of the brim with an awl or small nail. This will put tiny reference holes in the wood. When the pattern is removed, simply connect the "dots" with a pencil to establish the brim lines. Flip the head and pattern over and repeat this process. This method helps keep the hat lines consistent of both sides of the head. It works great for cowboys, and any other carvings wearing a hat!

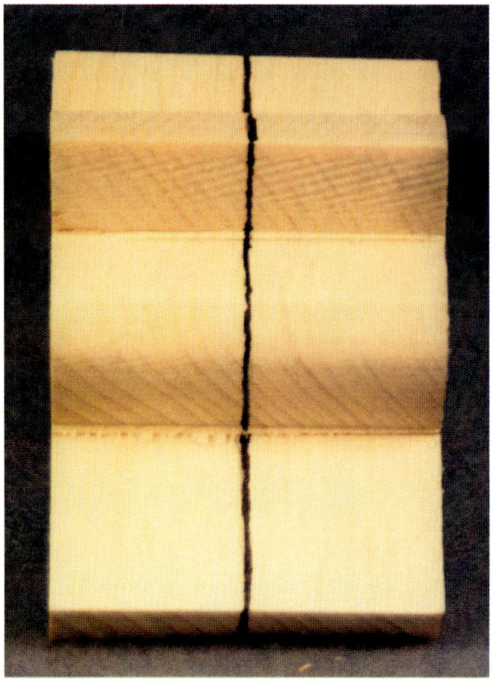

And down the back of the head.

Now, we need to set the overall width of the head, including the ears. This is an arbitrary call on your part, because you should vary these dimensions from carving to carving, so all your work doesn't look the same. For this project, I am going to come in from the left and right sides about 5/16". This will allow some of the hat brim to hang out over the head and ears. I have sketched in the lines as shown, to mark my reference points.

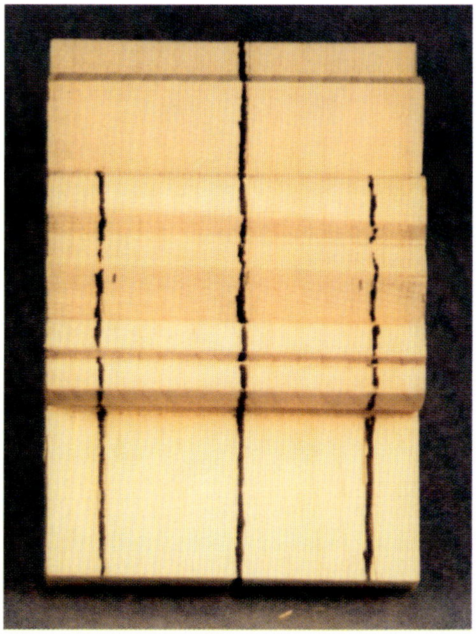

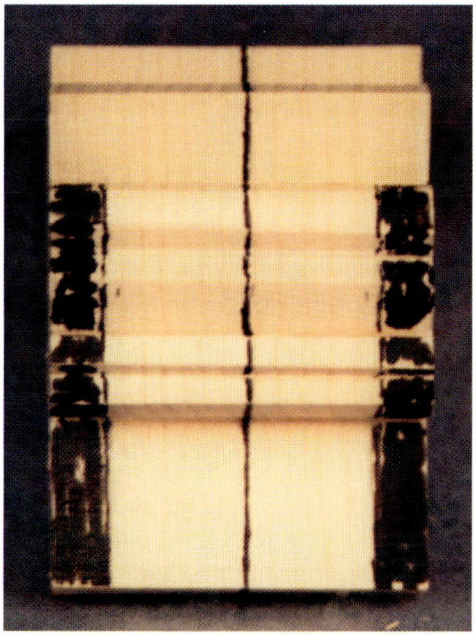

Our first goal is to remove the darkened sections of wood from the left and right sides of the head as follows:

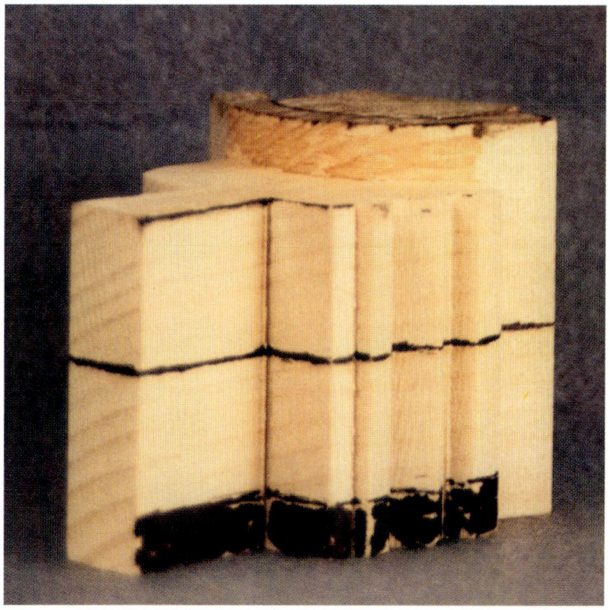

And here is the same side with wood removed up to the reference line. Our depth is now established on this side of the head.

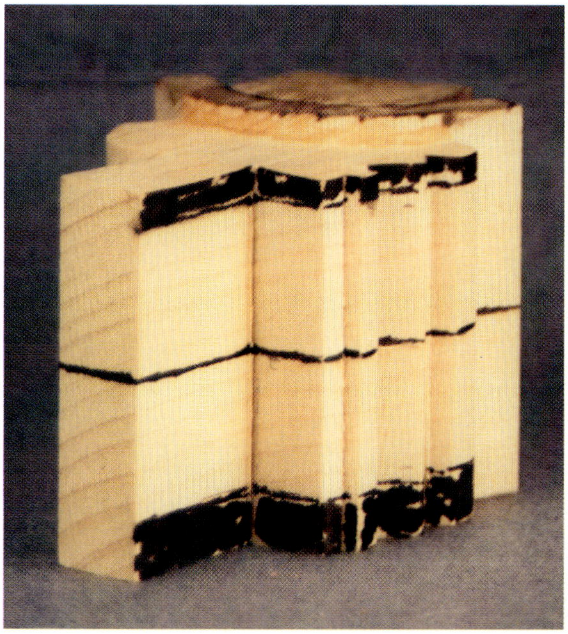

Using the tip of your knife, incise the lower brim line about 1/8" deep. Working up from the neck toward the brim, shave away the wood up to the "stop" cut you incised. You can use a knife or flat gouge for this process, whatever is easiest for you. Here is one side so far.

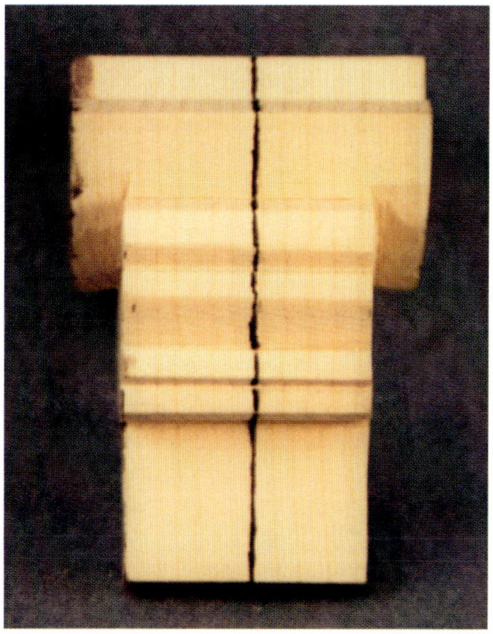

Repeat this process for the other side, and your head should look something like this. We'll come back and work on the hat, once we get the face, ears, and hair established. That way, we'll be able to carve the hat to a better fit.

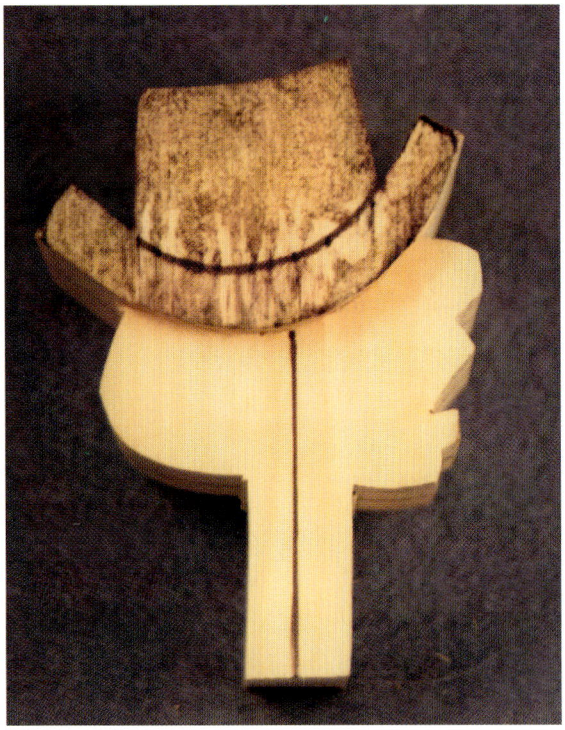

Sketch a vertical line down the approximate center of the head, as seen in this side view. This line will set the reference for the front of the ears. Do this on both sides of the head. **Note:** Don't panic! My wood hasn' t developed a blight. For many of the steps in the rest of the carving sequence, I will be staining the wood slightly, so you can more clearly see the wood I remove in a particular step. This will help you focus on a specific area, and not have to strain your eyes or patience, trying to figure out where I am carving in the photo.

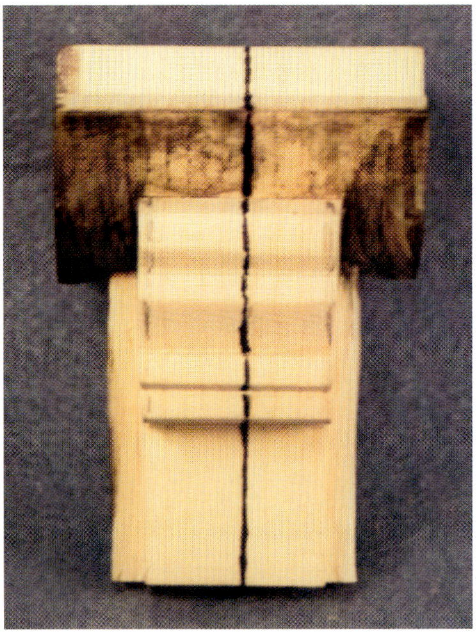

After doing both sides of the head, your carving should resemble this.

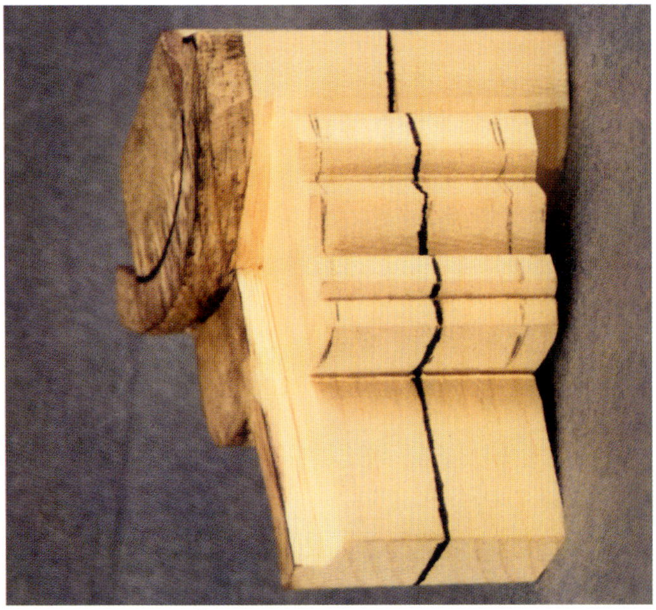

Incise the line with your knife tip, then use a knife or flat gouge to remove about 3/16" of wood. This establishes the width of the ear protrusion from the head.

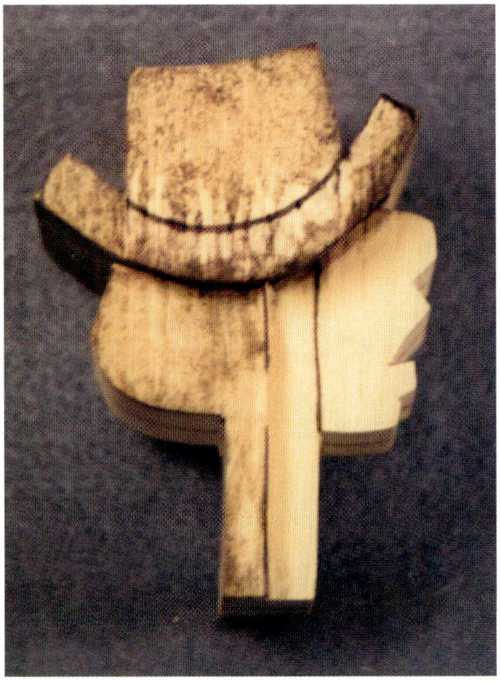

Now, sketch a vertical line even with the front of the neck. This will set the front edge of the sideburns. Do this on both sides of the head.

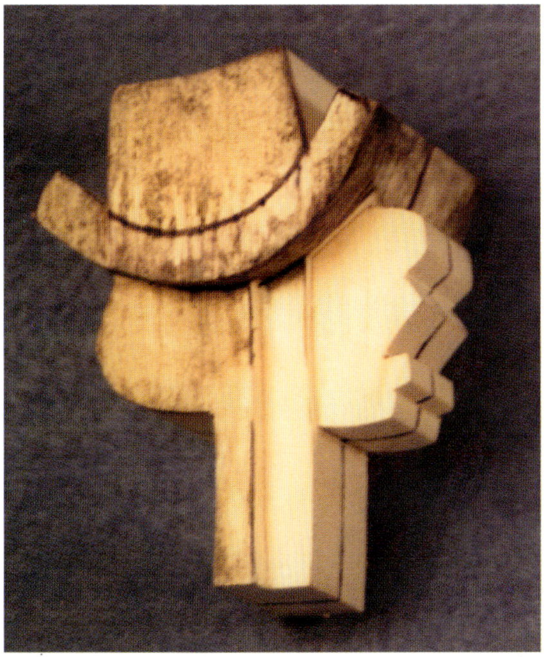

Incise the line with your knife tip, then use a knife or flat gouge to remove about 1/8" of wood. This sets the thickness of the sideburns, as seen in this view.

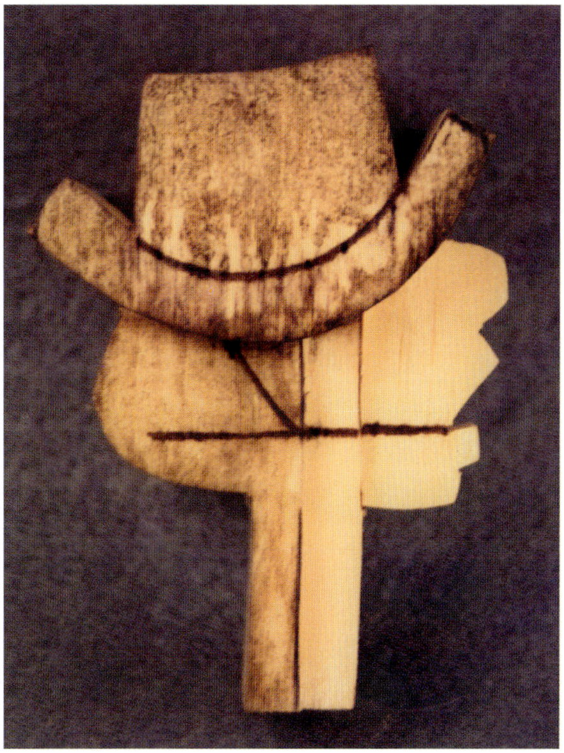

Now, complete a triangle as shown by the additional line from the bottom of the horizontal line up toward the rear of the head. This establishes the rough dimensions of the ear. For this project, the top of my ears are about 5/16" wide. Again, do this on both sides of the head.

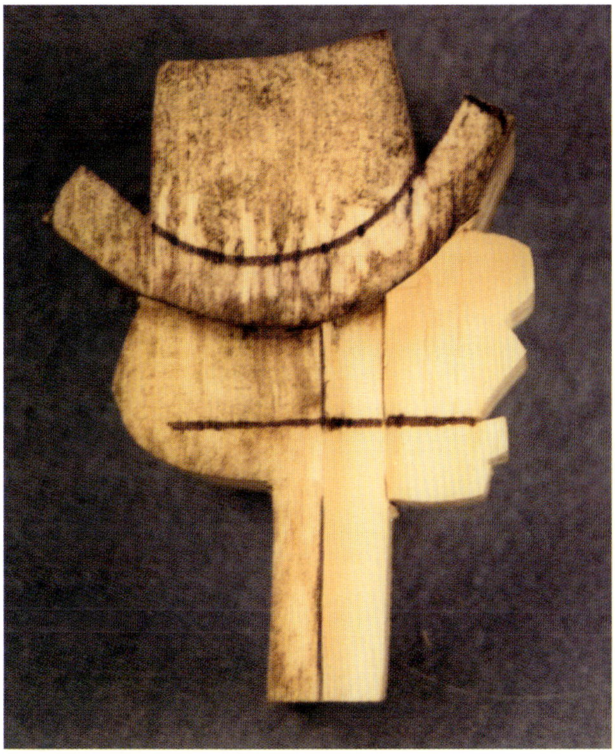

Sketch a horizontal line across the head, even with the back of the mouth. This will set the bottom of the ears. Do this on both sides of the head.

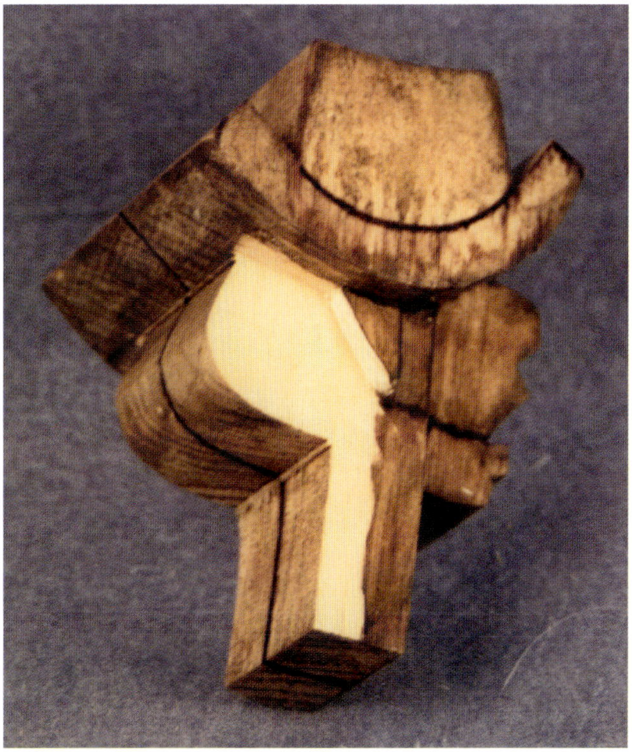

Now, use your knife to incise the rear line, then remove wood once more to a depth of about 3/16". (This should make the rear of the head even with the sideburn thickness in front). You have now set the rear of the ear protrusion. **Note:** From this point on, if I tell you to remove wood on one side of the head, body, etc., do it on both sides.

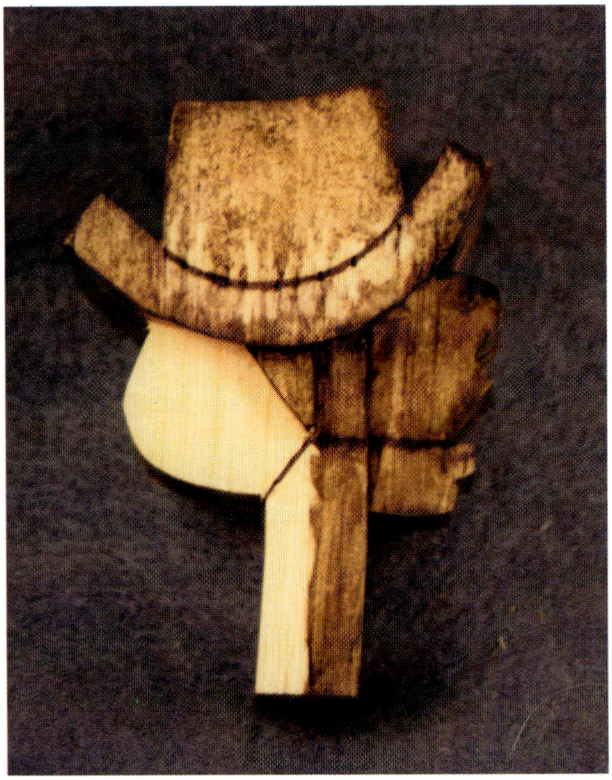

Sketch a line from the bottom of the ear to the rear top corner of the neck. This will define the hairline in back of the ear.

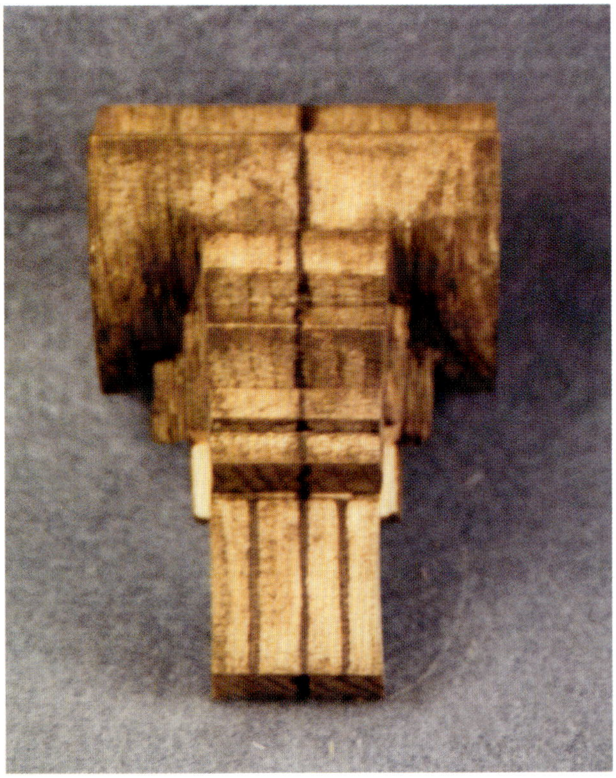

Next, sketch two vertical lines down the front of the neck, about halfway between the centerline and the outside edges of the neck. This will establish the approximate width of the neck.

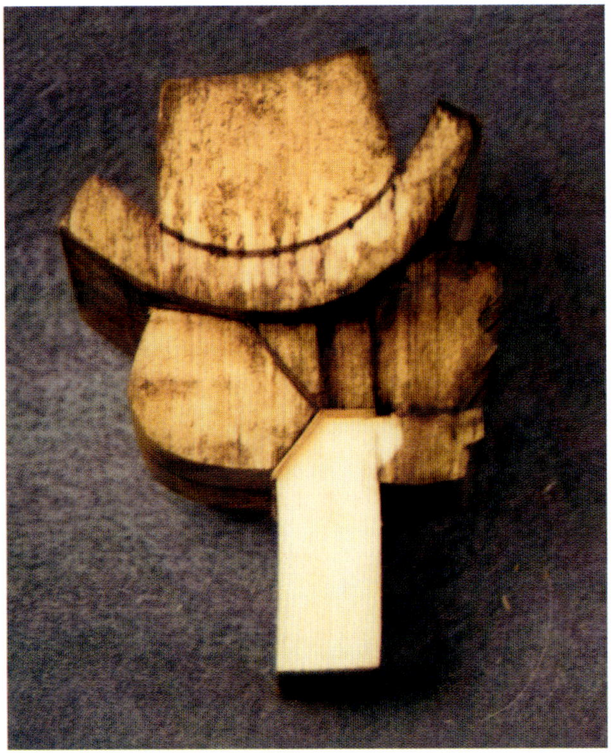

Incise the line with your knife, then remove wood until this entire section is even with the thickness of the face, as seen here.

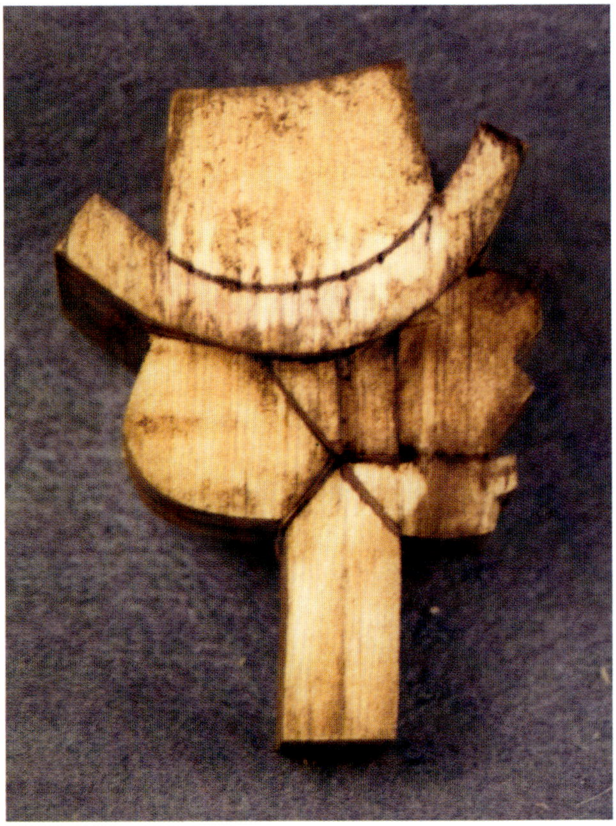

Establish the jaw line by sketching a line from the bottom of the ear to the upper front corner of the neck.

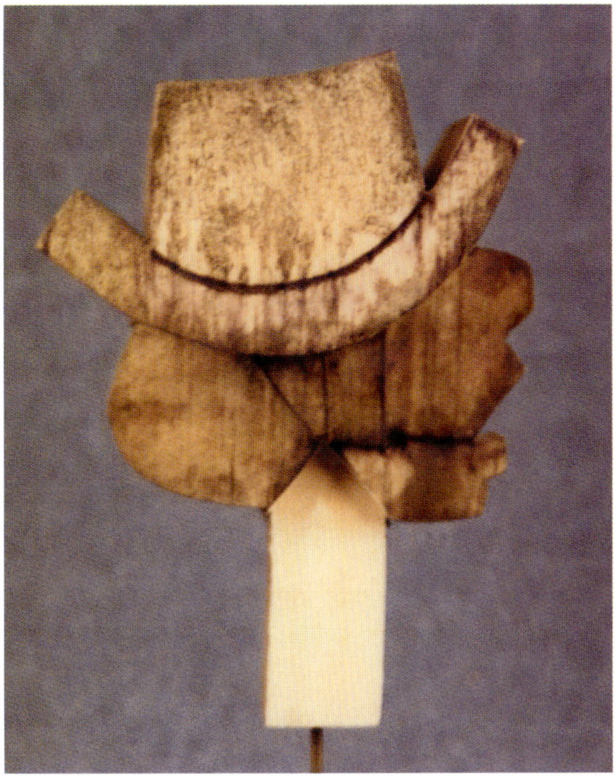

Incise the line, and remove wood until you reach the depth established by the vertical lines you sketched on the front of the neck. Here is a side view so far....

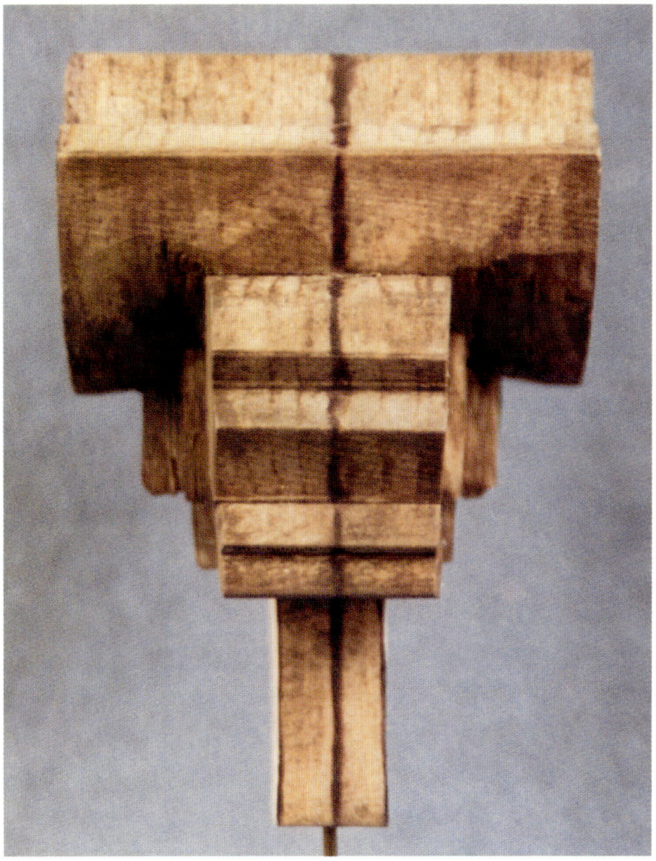

The neck has now been reduced in width to the vertical

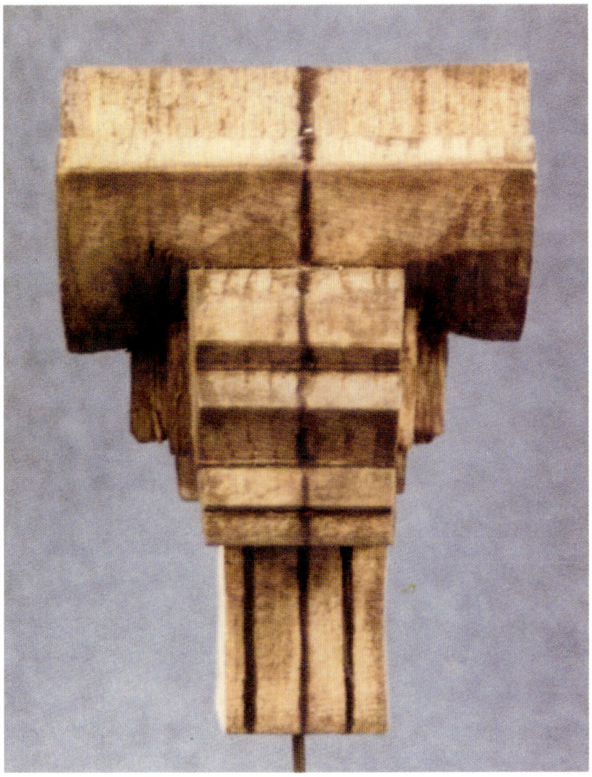

And here is a front view so far.

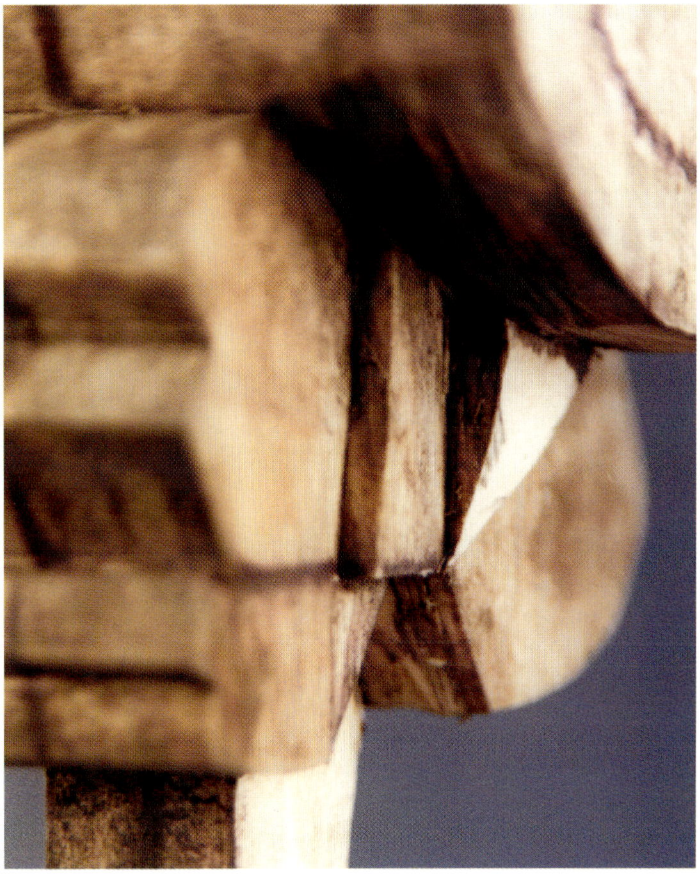

Starting at the top of the ear, use your knife to shave downward so that the ears protrude at the top, and taper to be nearly flush with the sideburns at the bottom.

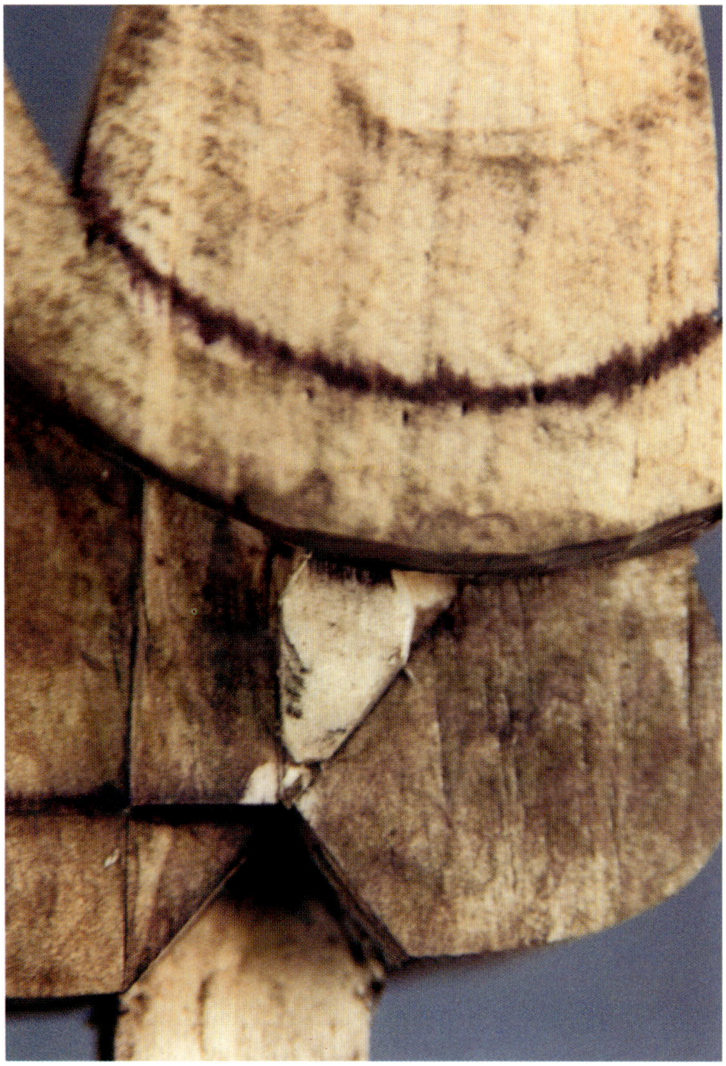

Remove the sharp corners from the ears using your knife. Repeat as necessary until you are happy with the roundness of the ears.

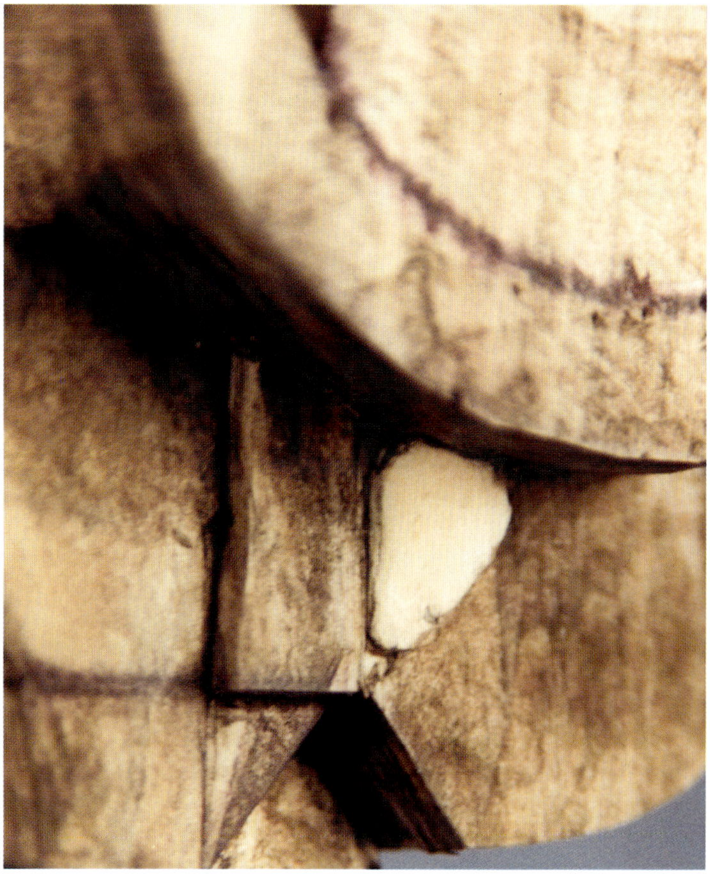

Use your knife to shave away the sharp edge on the front of the ears at about a 45° angle, up and down the front edge (from the front edge of the ear to the back edge). By putting a taper on the ear in this direction, it is easier to gouge away the wood in the next step without splintering the ear.

Use a 10mm "U" gouge to remove wood from the inside of the ear, cutting in from the rear edge of the ear, toward the side-burns, as seen here. Then, to finish the ear, use your knife to gently remove any sharp edges that still remain.

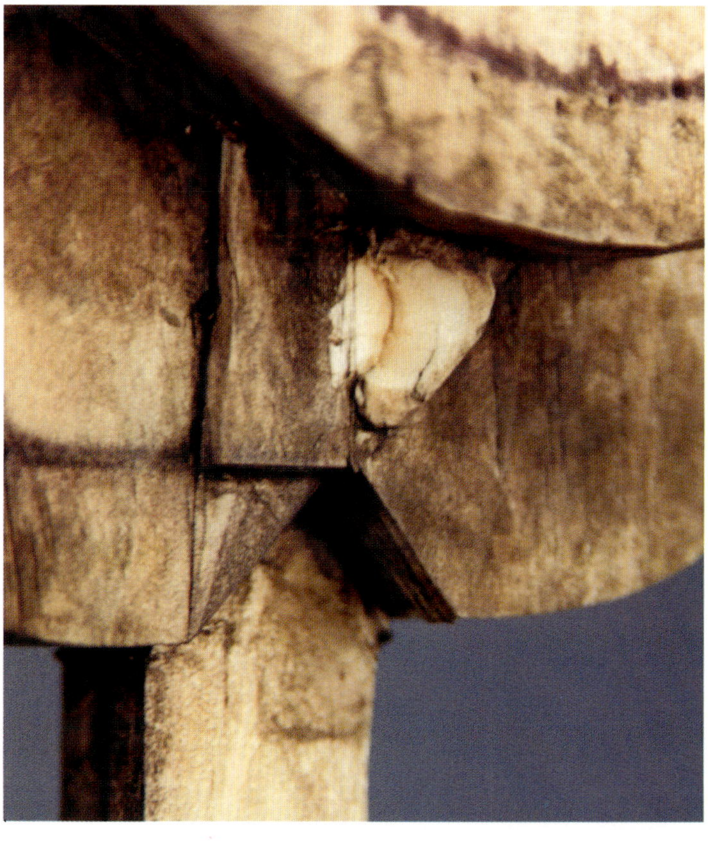

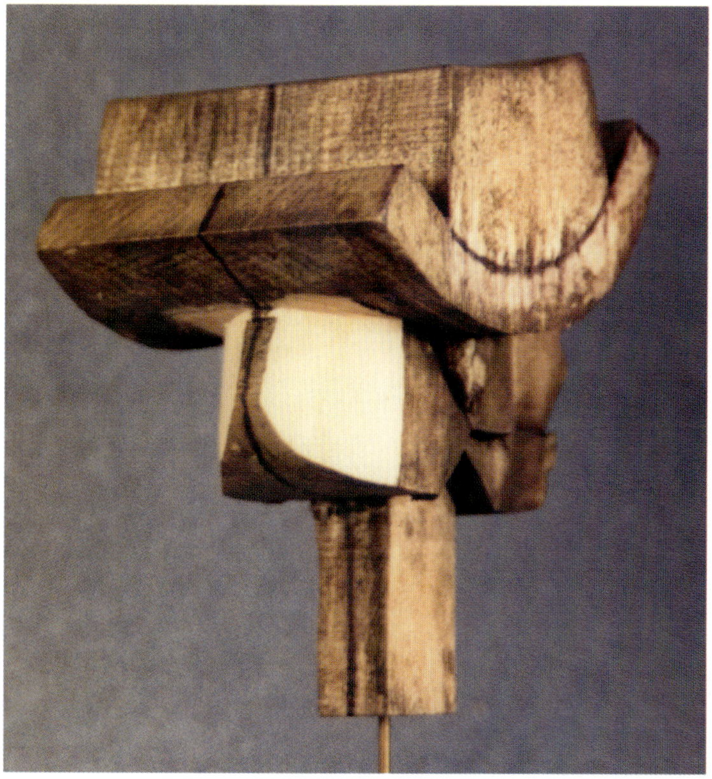

Now, use your knife to knock off the rear corners of the head.

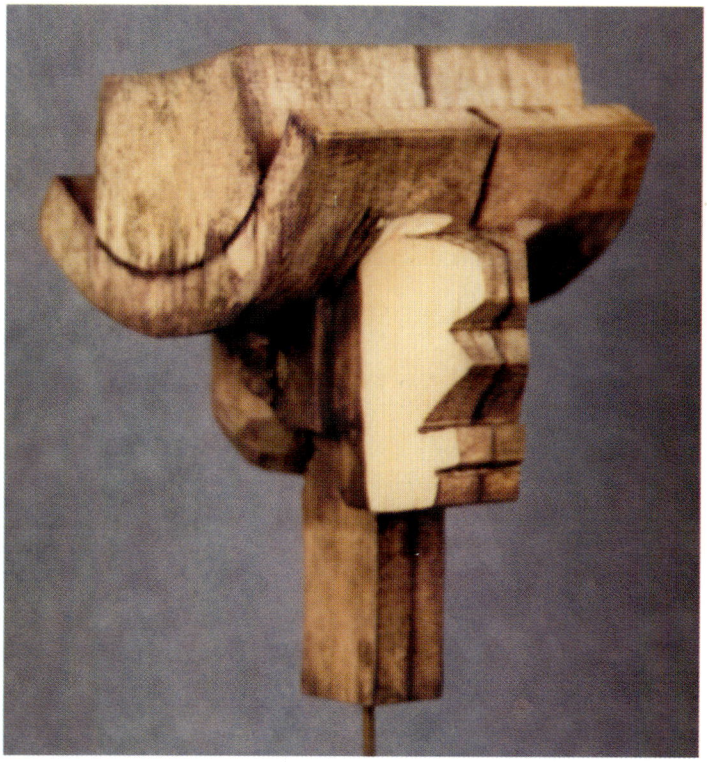

Remove the two sharp corners on the front of the face, at about a 45° angle, using your knife. Then, use your knife to round off any new sharp edges this step produced. You want a fairly round face, from the outer edges of the nose around to the sideburns.

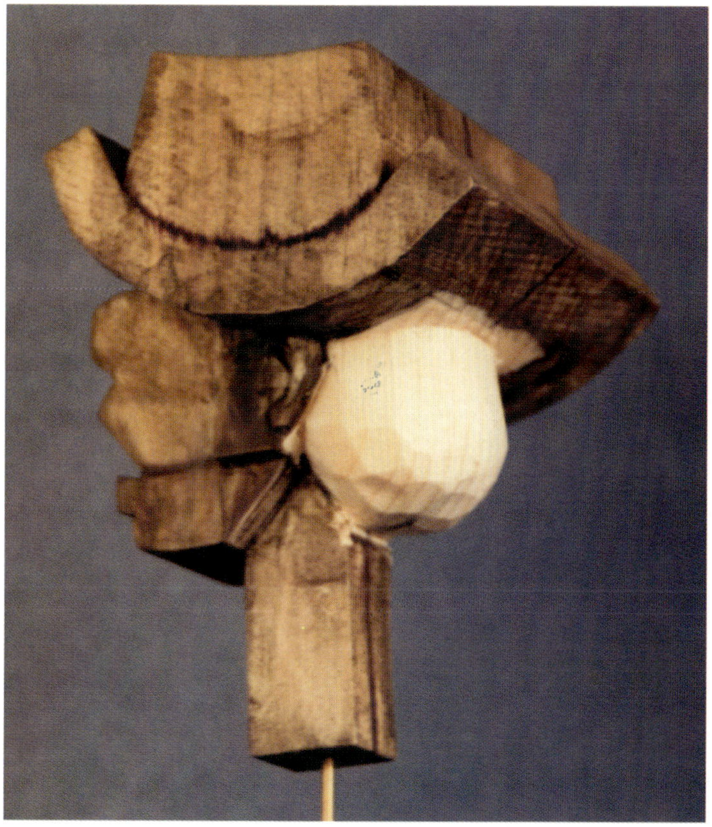

Next, round off the sharp edges on the rear of the head and hair, but don't carve on the neck yet.

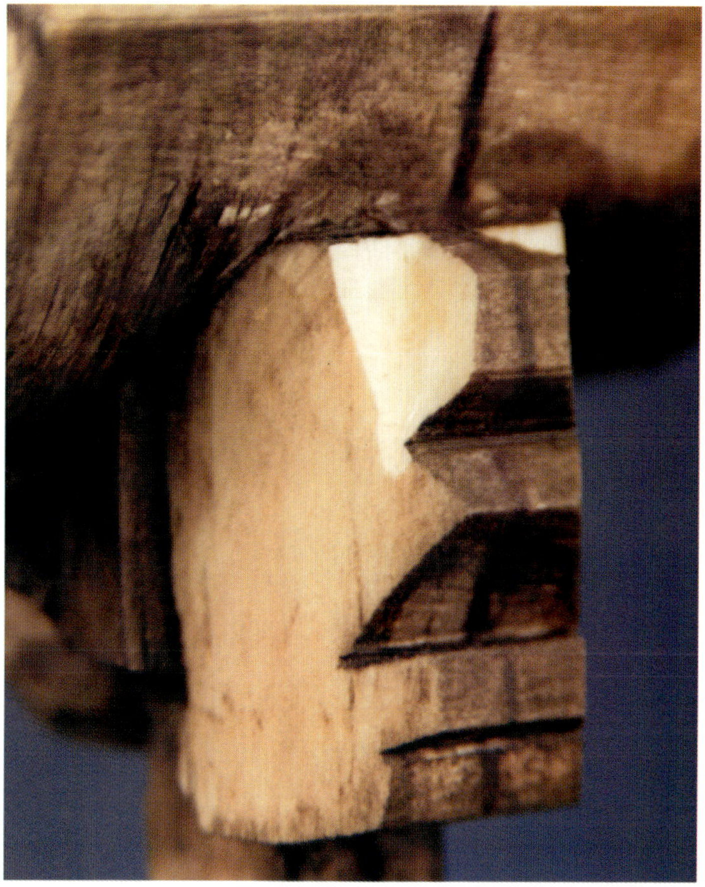

To define the nose, use a 1/4" "V" gouge to cut a slanted groove from the bottom of the nose, up to the hat, tapering in toward the center of the nose as you reach the top.

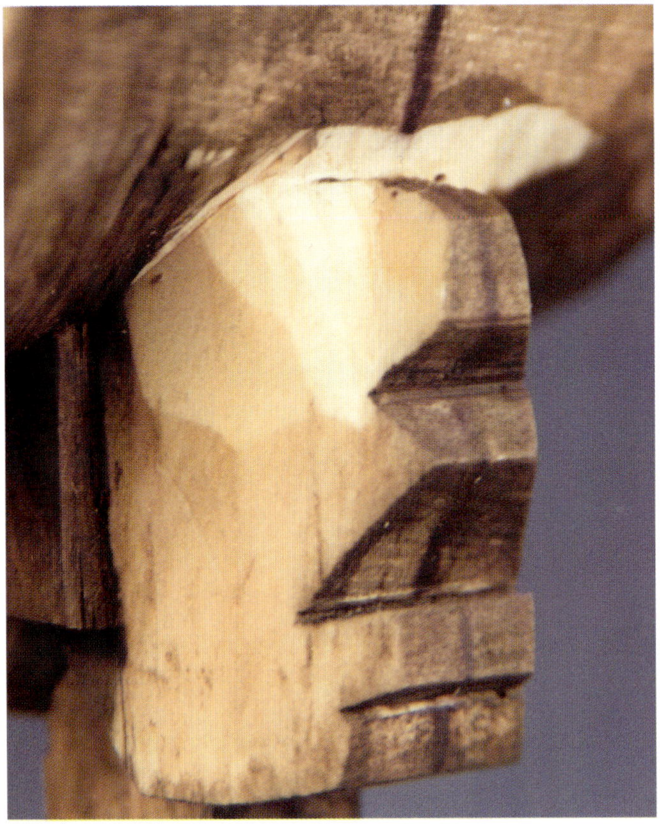

Use your knife to round off the face area on each side of the

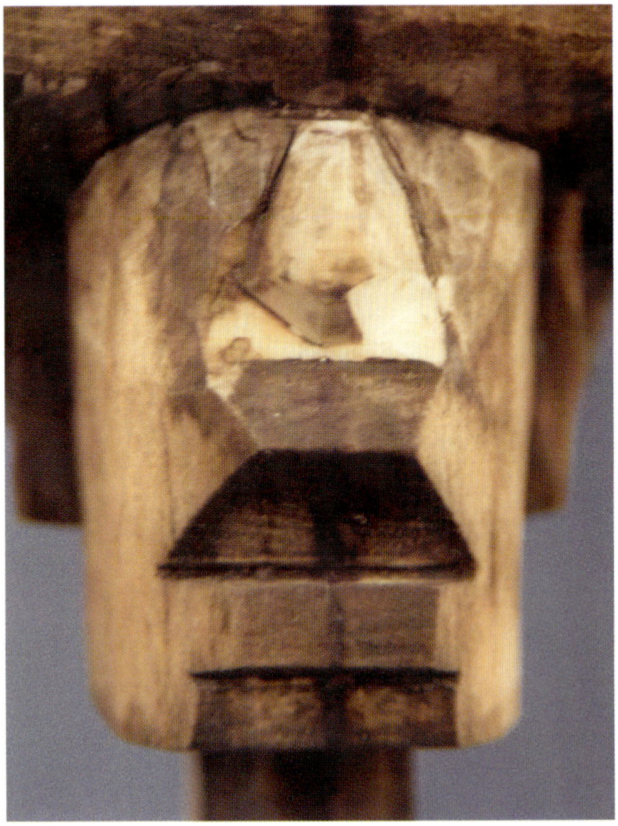

Next, clip off the bottom outside corners of the nose at about a 45° angle, using your knife. Then, round off any sharp edges this step produced.

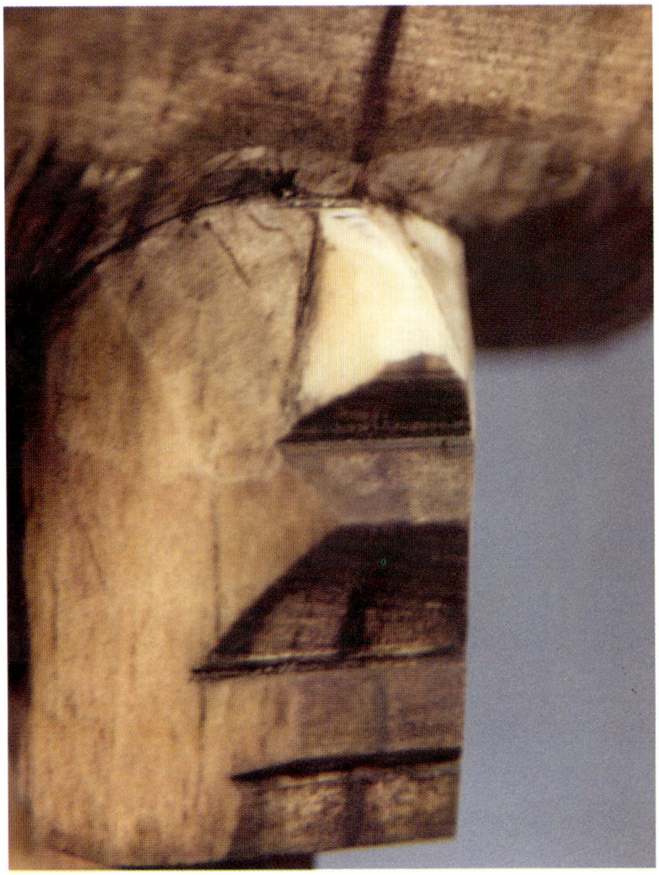

Round off the sharp edges on the front of the nose.

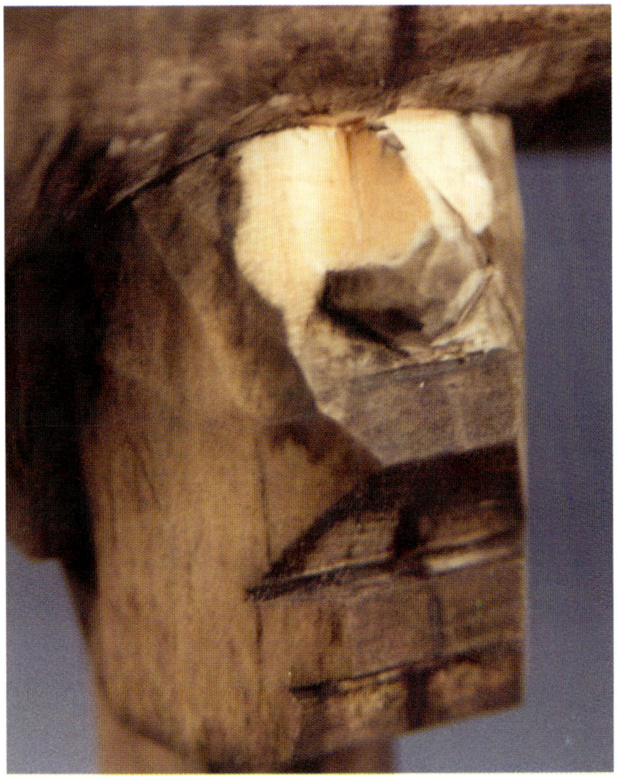

To create a nostril flare, go about 1/8" above the lower edge of the nose, and scoop in and up with your knife. Removing this section of wood will cause the lower part of the nose to be wider, and the upper part to be narrower. (You may also need to shave in from the face toward the nose in order to get this section of wood released).

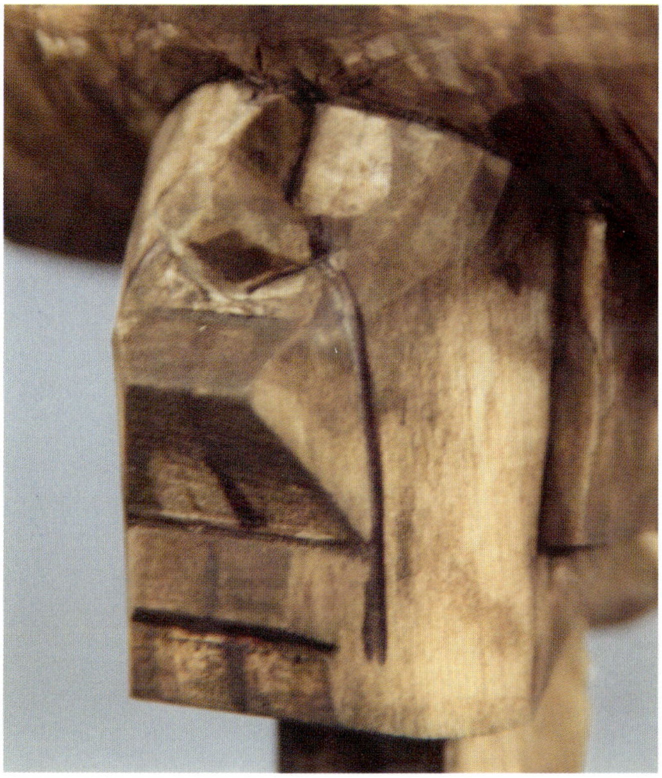

Sketch a line from the lower outside edge of the nose, down past the outer edge of the mouth, to the bottom of the lower lip.

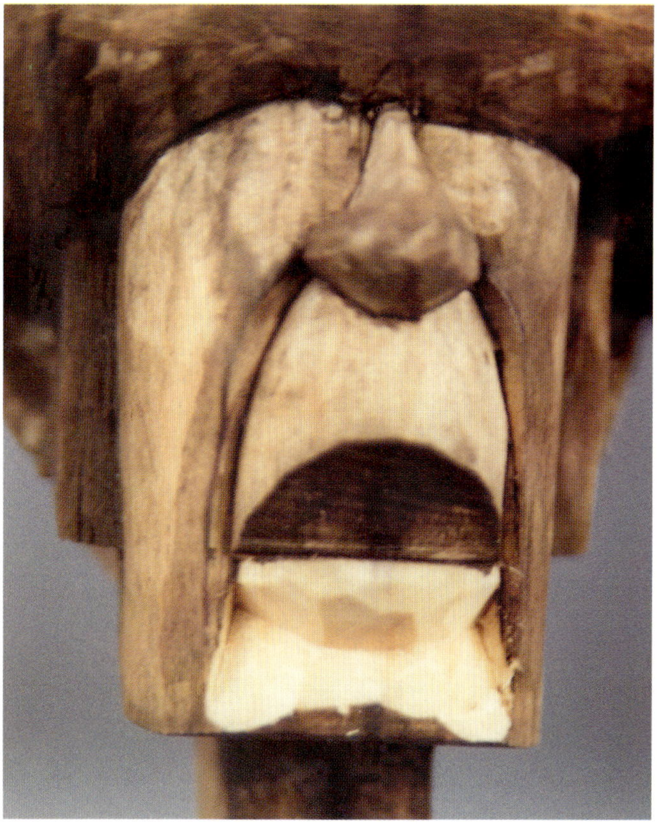

Now, incise along the bottom of the lower lip, from the center of the mouth all the way to the lines you incised at the outside edges of the mouth. Use your knife to remove wood so the

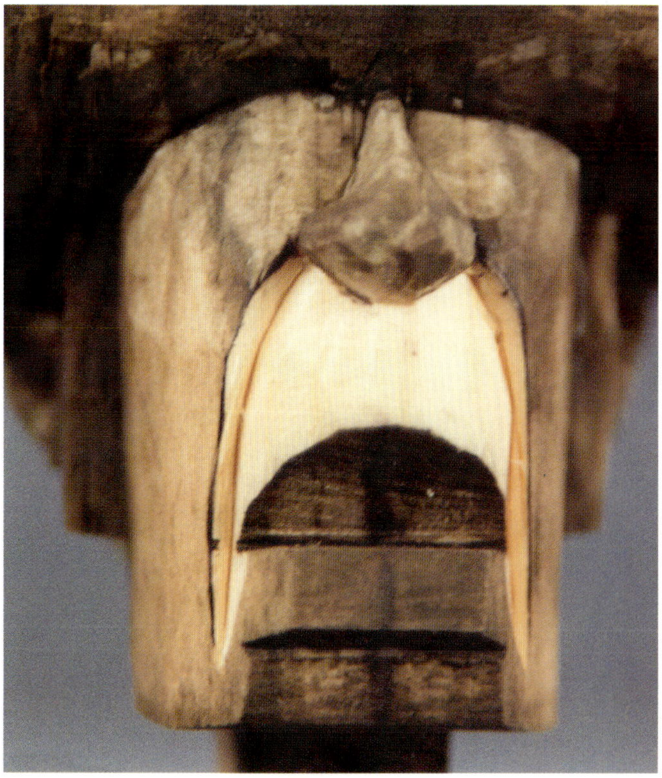

Incise these lines about 1/8" deep with your knife. Then, working from the center of the face out toward each line, remove wood with your knife to form the mouth mound.

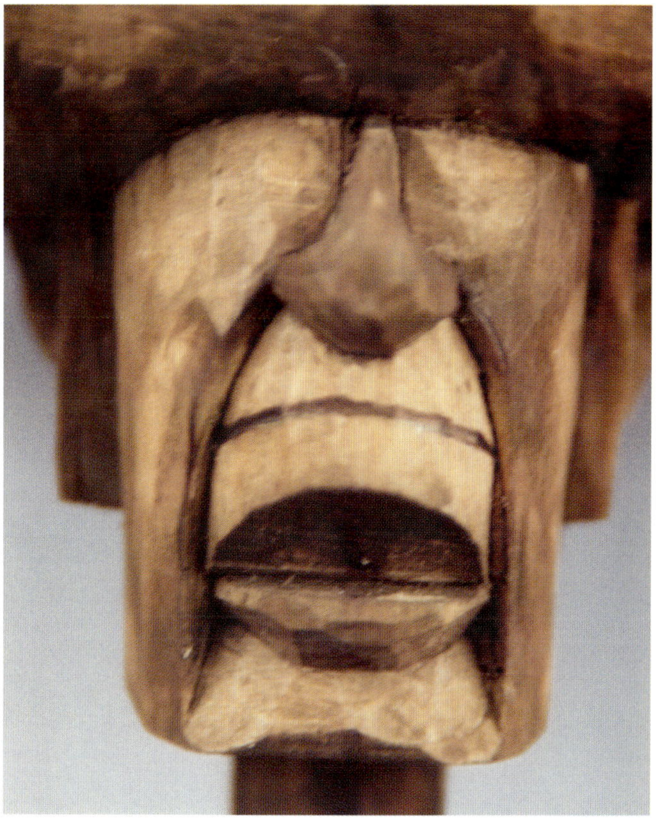

Ol' Hurricane is a happy guy, so we need to give him teeth for a big old smile. Sketch a line to define the separation between the upper lip and the teeth.

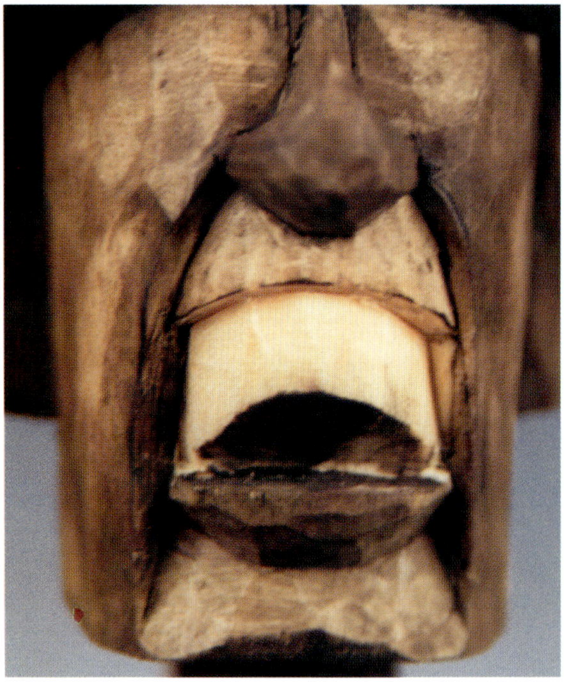

Incise the line about 1/8" deep with your knife tip. Working from the tooth section, shave upward toward the incision. When the wood is removed, this will cause the upper lip to stand out from the teeth.

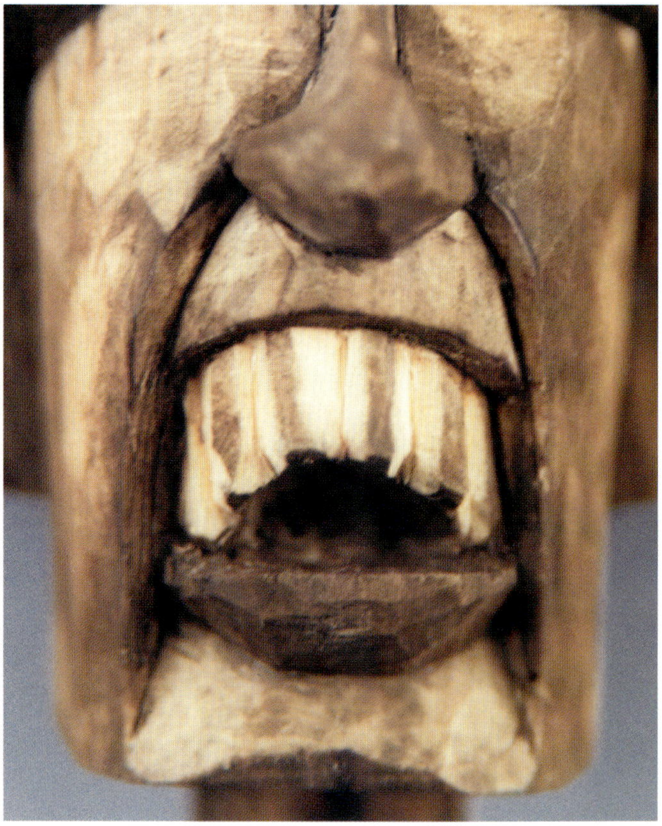

Now, incise vertical lines about 1/16" deep in the teeth. Space them about 1/8" apart, or whatever looks funny to you. Using your knife, shave toward the vertical incisions from both sides, so that a "V"-shaped section of wood is removed. This adds a bit of detail to the teeth, and makes them more realistic and humorous.

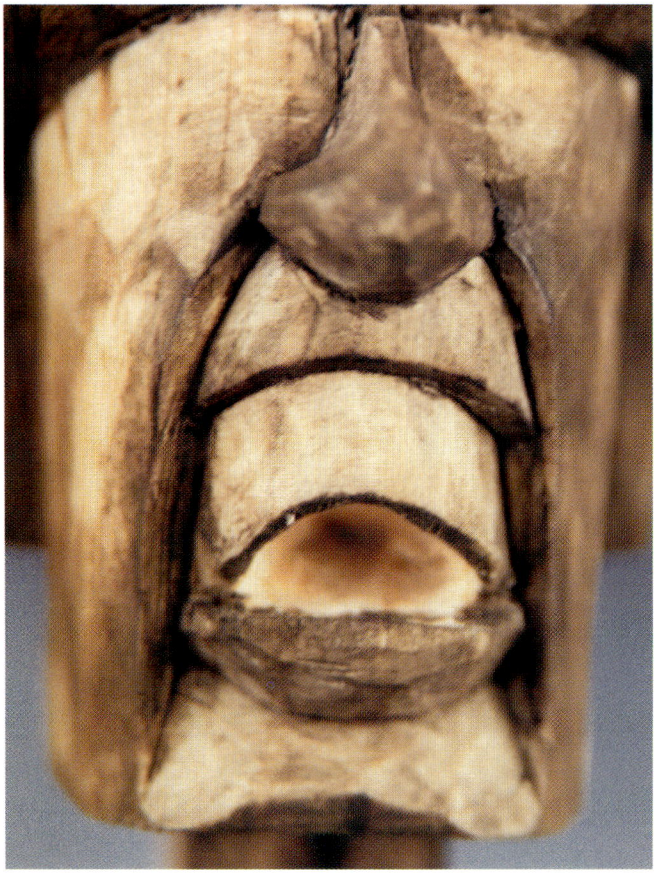

Use a 5mm "U" gouge to remove wood from the inside of the mouth. You don't have to drill to China, just go deep enough so that the inside of the mouth will have some definition.

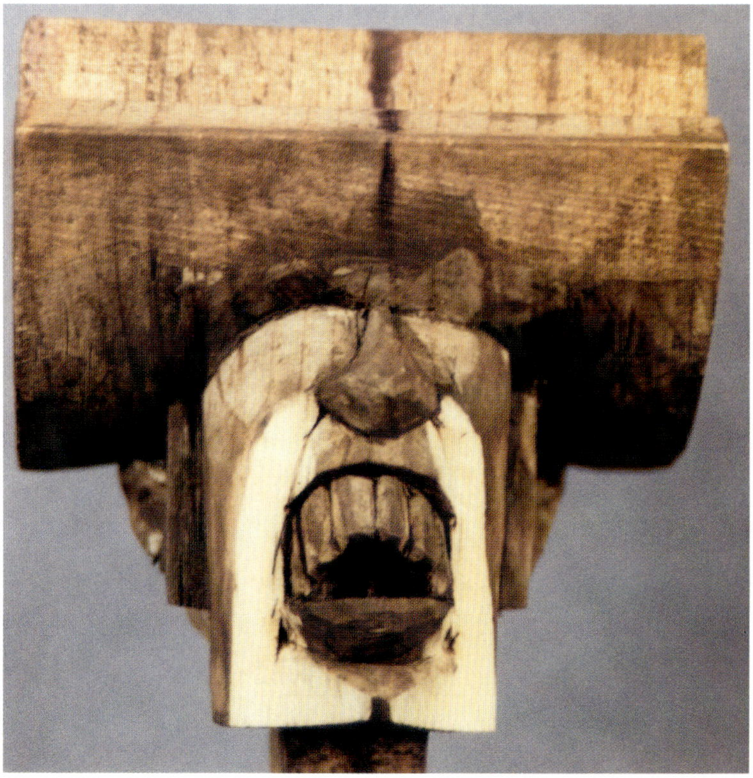

Let's finish shaping the lower part of the face. Using your knife, remove the sharp edges on the wood running down both sides of the mouth. Notice the chin area. It has more of a pointed shape now.

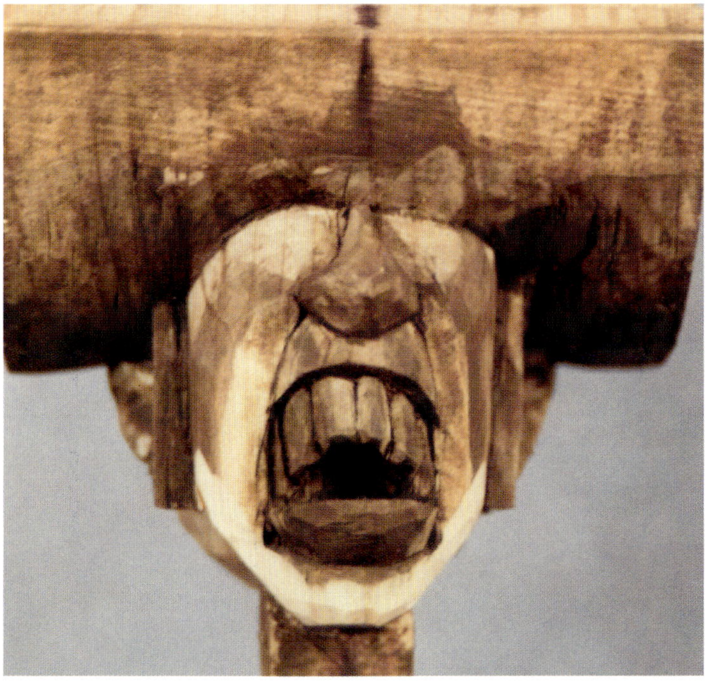

Now, round off the lower edge of the face, but don't carve on the neck yet.

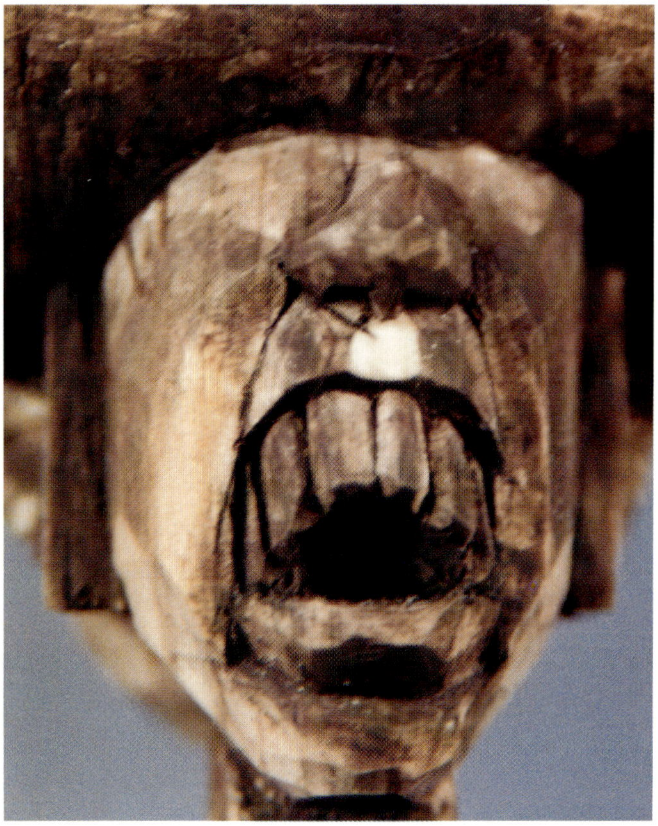

Use a 5mm "U" gouge to make a small depression on the upper lip, centered under the nose.

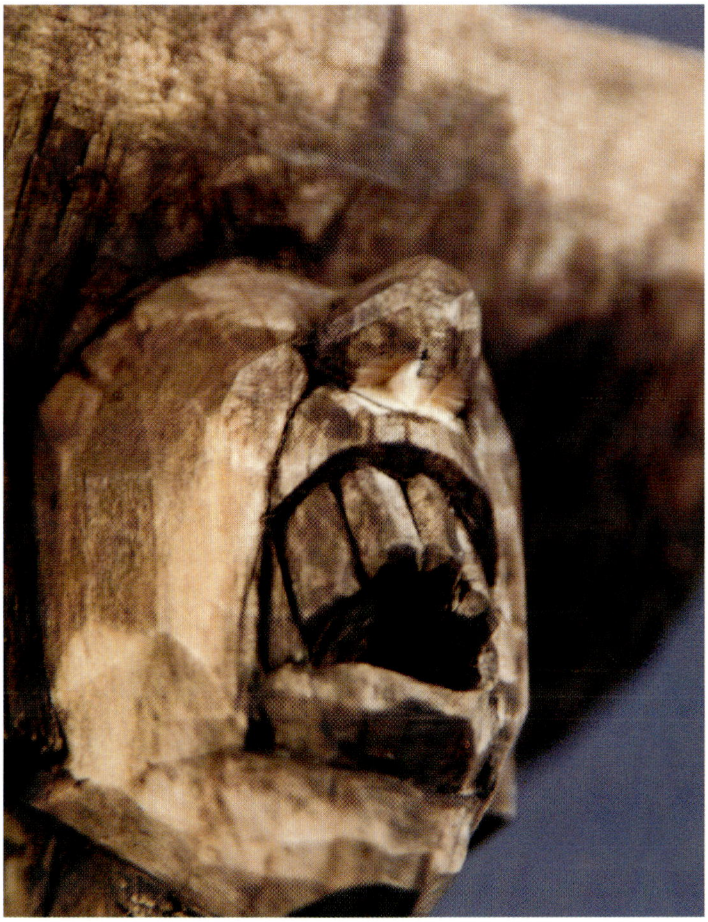

To create nostrils, use the tip of your knife to notch out and remove two triangular-shaped pieces of wood from the bottom of the nose.

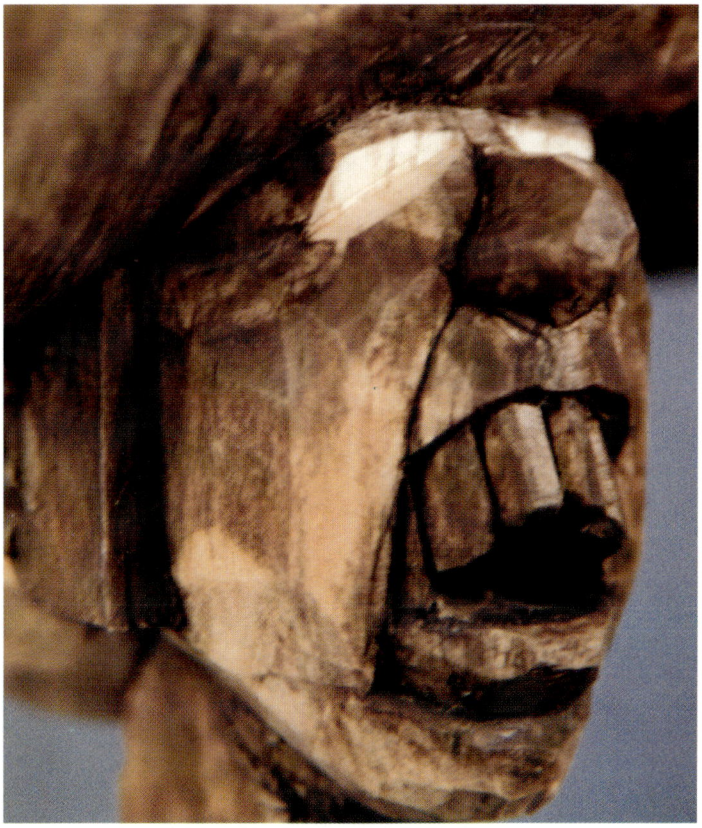

Use your knife or 1/8" "V" gouge to cut a "V"-shaped groove in the face, on each side of the nose, near the top. Since the hat is worn so low, we won't try to make detailed eyeballs or eyebrows. We'll paint these grooves later to add some simple eye detail.

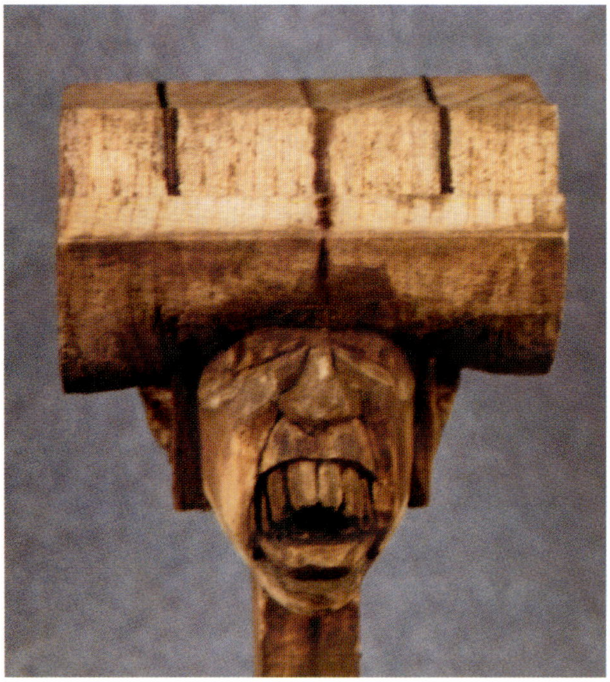

Now that the face and head are shaping up, let's do some work on the hat. To set the width of the crown, look at the hat from the front. Imagine lines projecting up the head, even with the outside of the sideburns. Sketch in these lines on the crown, in front and back. (Carry the lines over the top and rear of the crown to keep things lined up).

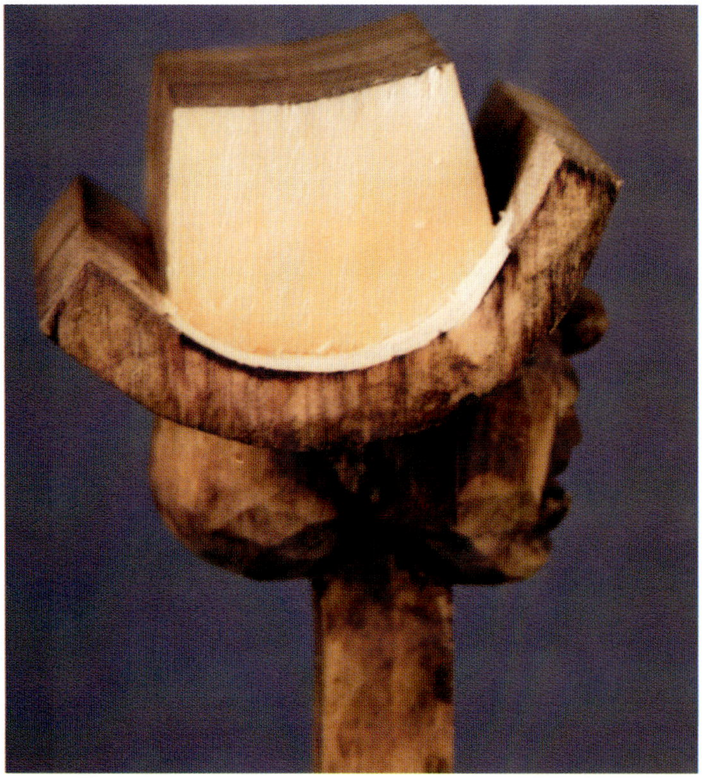

Working from the side, incise the upper line on the brim, which also is the bottom of the crown. Use your knife or 1/2" straight gouge to remove wood to the depth established by the vertical lines you drew in the previous step.(NOTE: If you have a curved gouge which closely resembles the lower curve of the crown, this is the best one to use to make the wood removal easy. This is a side view of one side completed.....

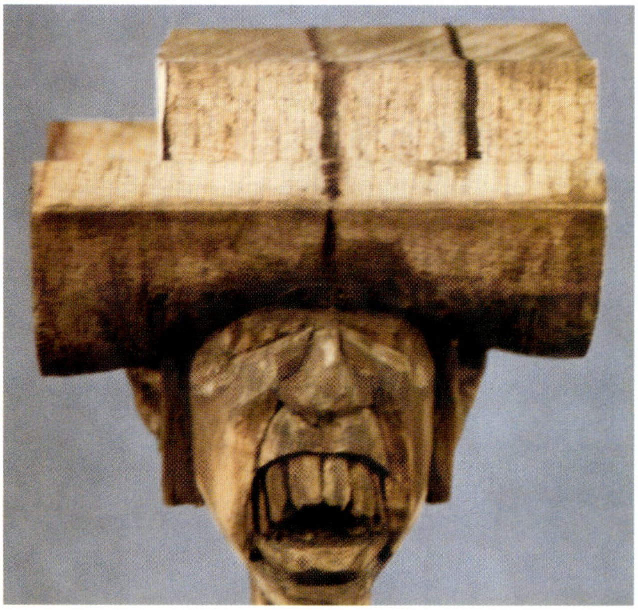

And here is a front view of one side done.

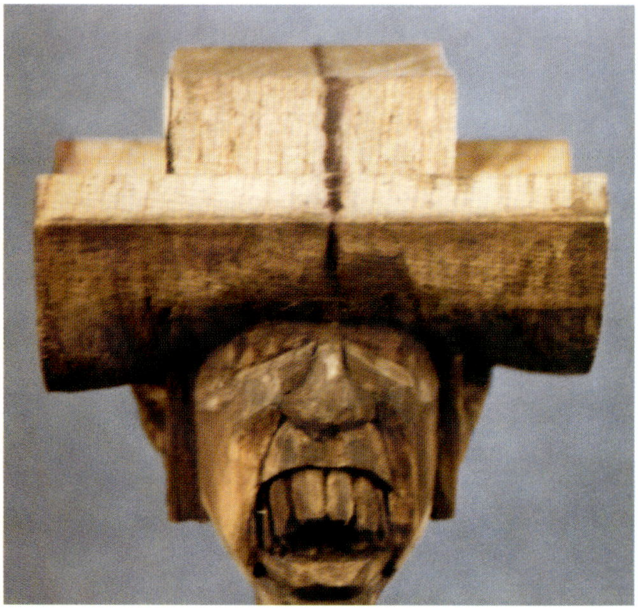

A front view of both sides done...

And a rear view of both sides done.

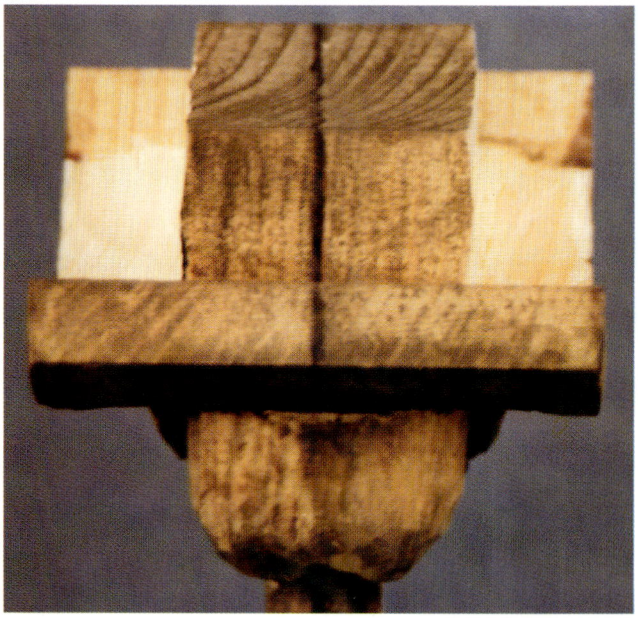

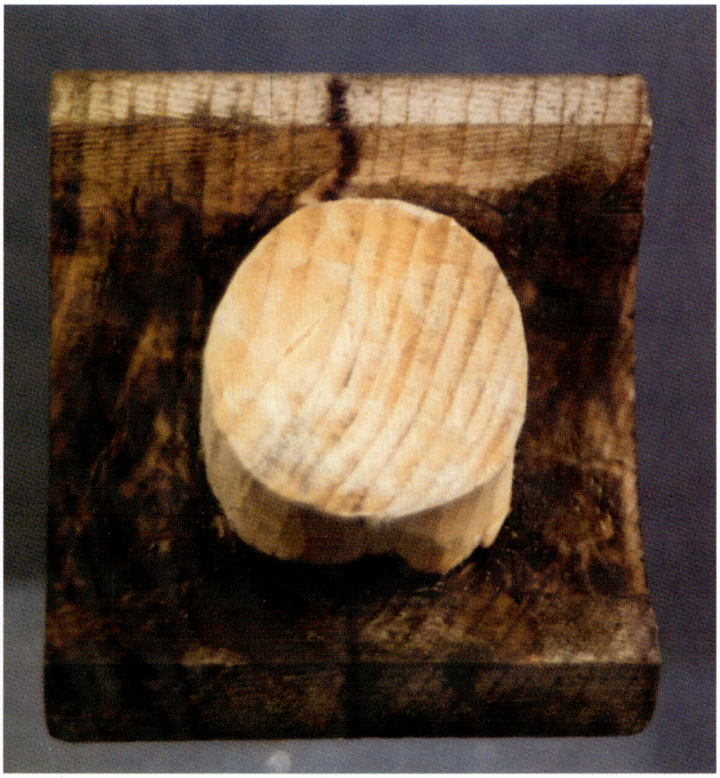

Now that the rough dimensions of the crown are established, remove the sharp edges, and keep removing sharp edges until the crown has assumed a fairly round shape, as seen in this top view.

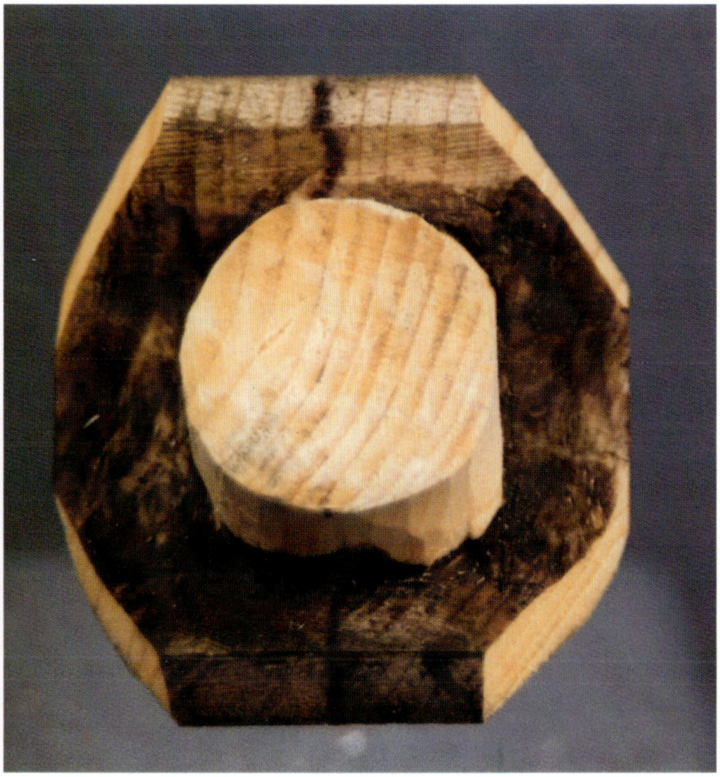

Next, use your knife to bring the brim into a round shape. First, knock off the four sharp corners as seen in this top view.

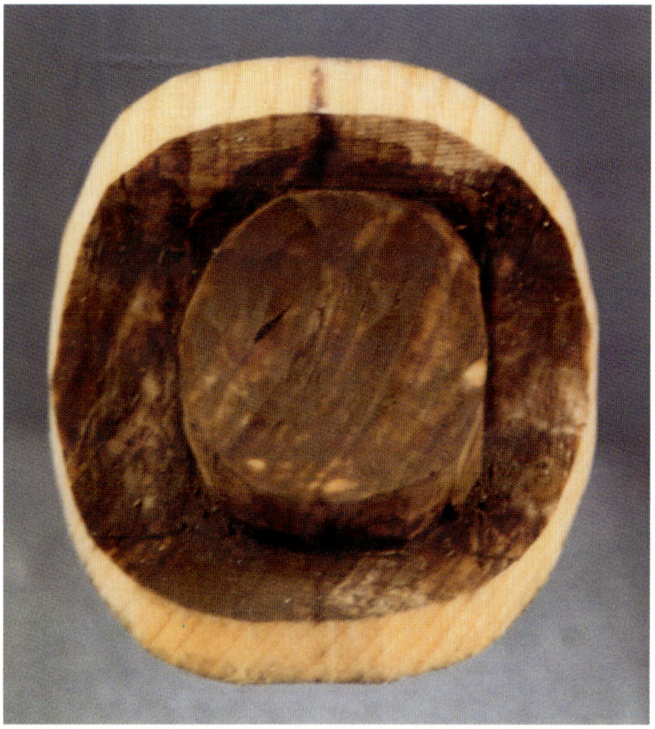

Keep rounding off the sharp edges until the brim is nice and round, as seen here.

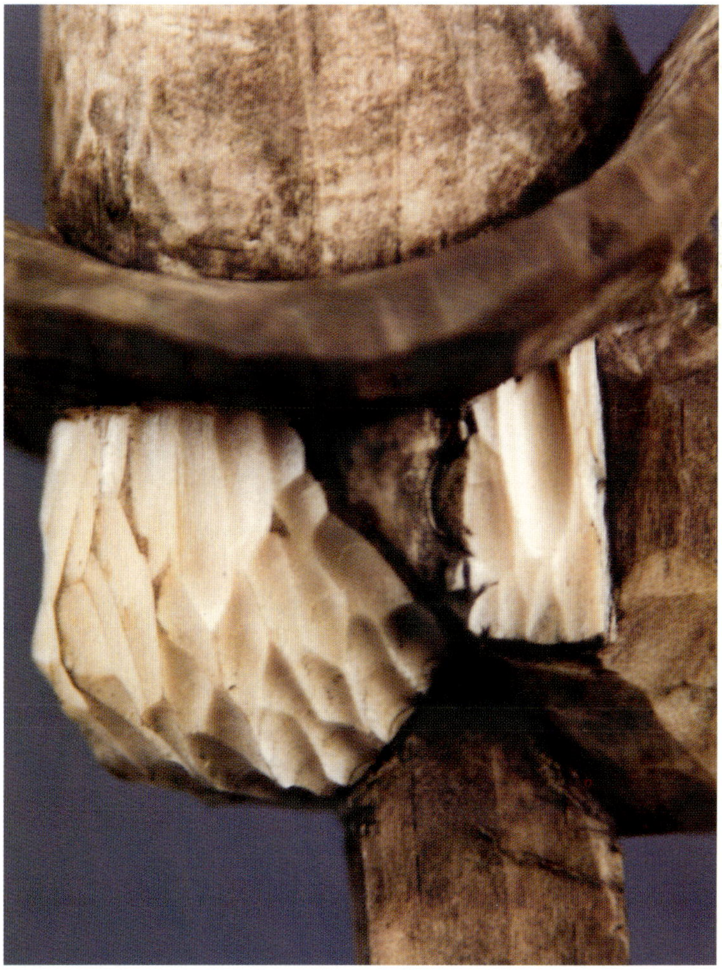

Use a 3mm "U" gouge to add detail to the sideburns and hair behind the ears.

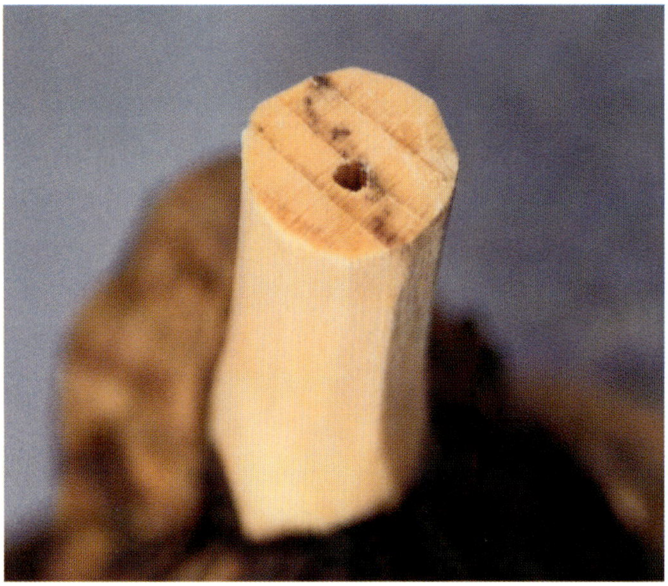

Use your knife to remove the four sharp edges from the neck, then keep removing sharp edges until the neck is round, as seen in this bottom view. We'll adjust the length of the neck later, as required.

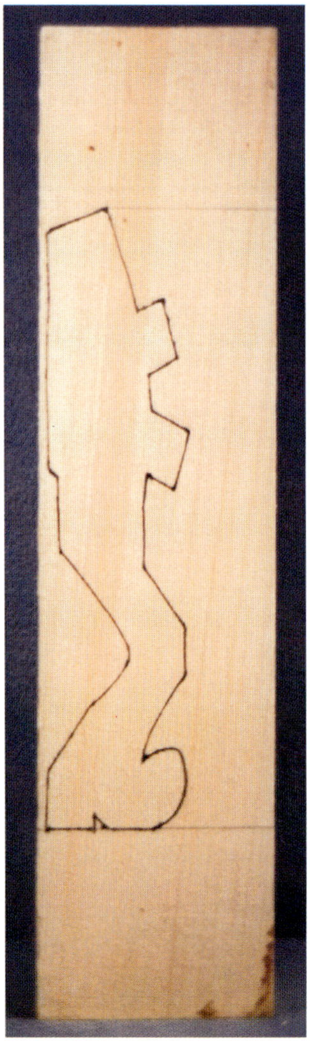

Transfer the side view of the body to a section of 3" x 3" wide wood.

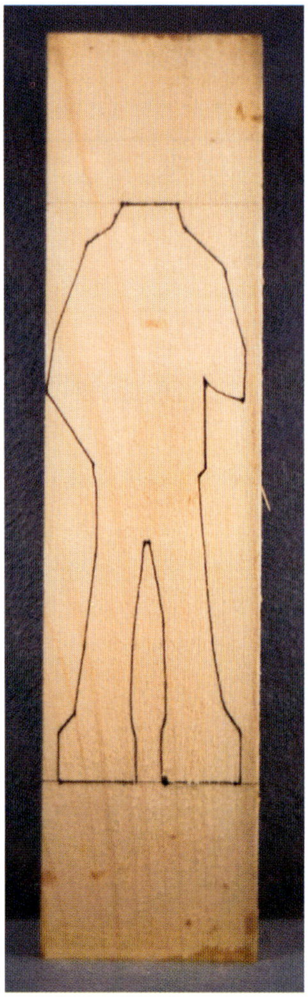

Next, transfer the front view to the wood.

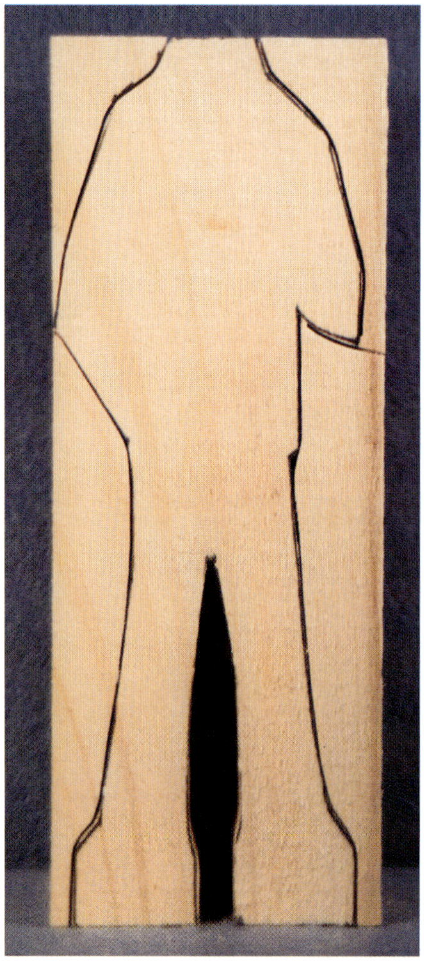

Saw the wood from between the legs. Also, partially saw on the other lines, but do not saw the wood completely away from the left and right sides yet.

Saw out the side profile.

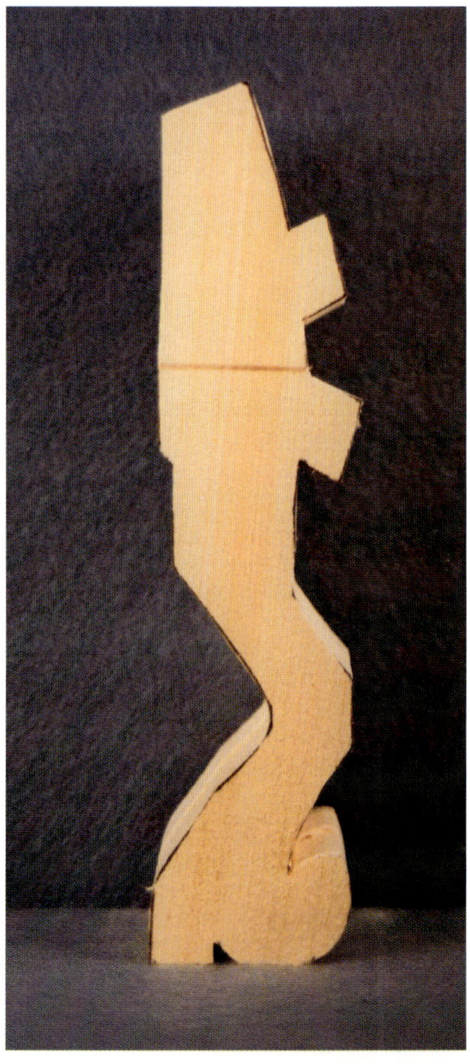

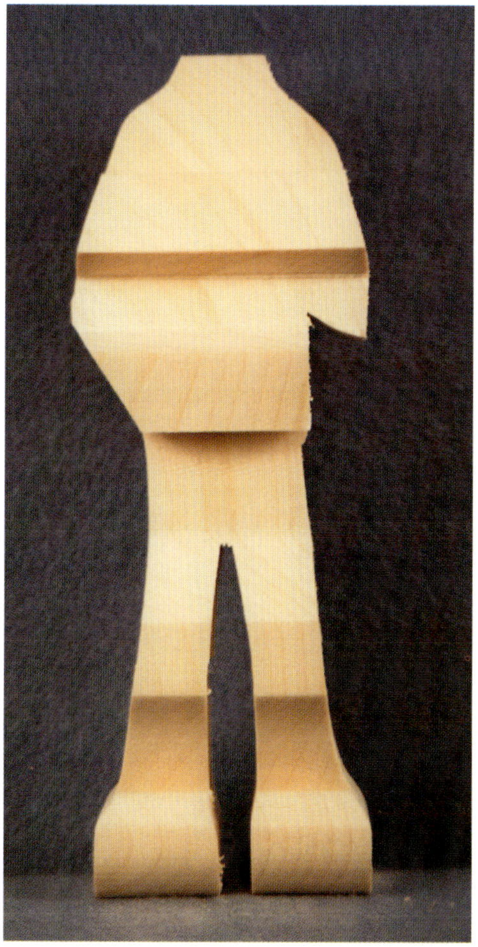

Now go ahead and finish sawing out the front profile.

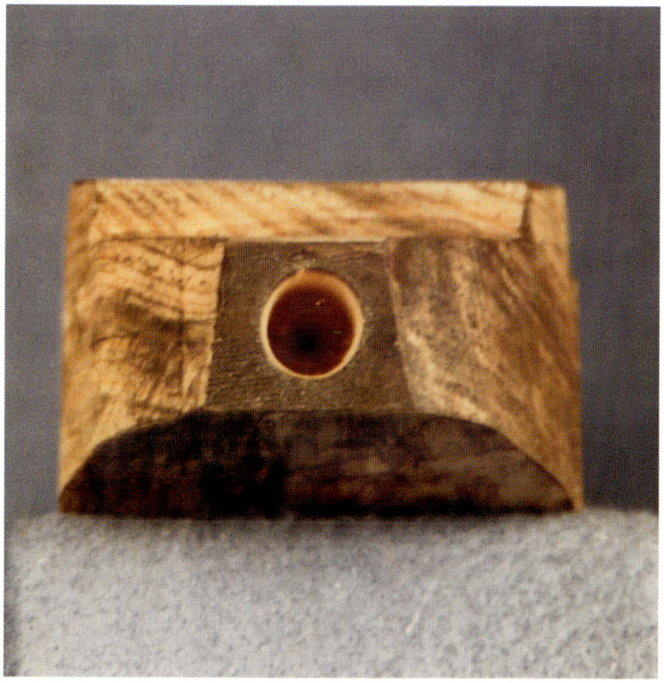

Using a drill bit that is slightly larger than the diameter of the neck, drill about 3/4" deep into the top center of the body, in order to make a hole to receive the head later. (You can trim down the thickness of the neck, if needed, until you get a match between the neck size and your available drill bits).

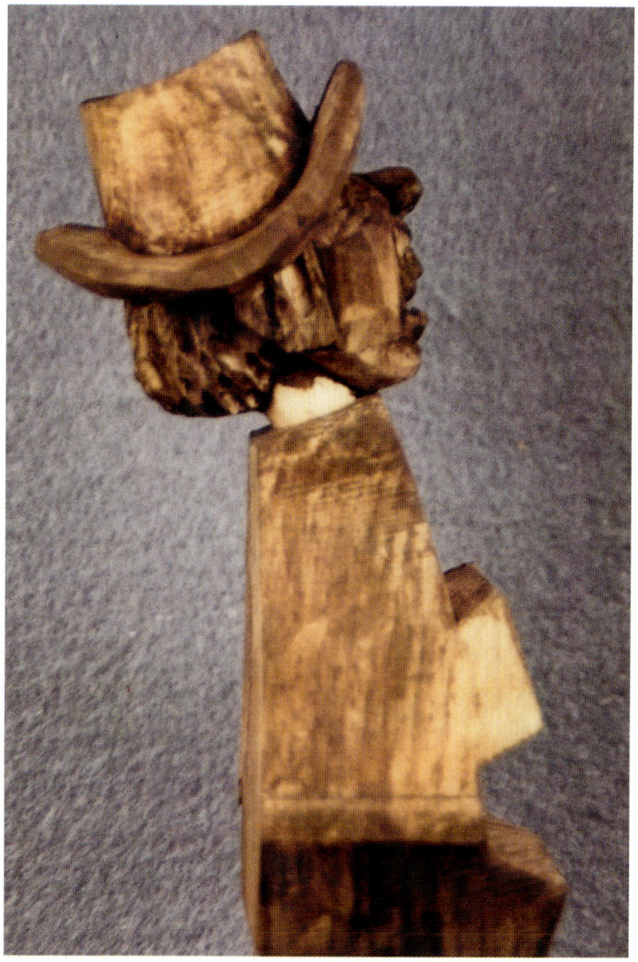

Test-fit the head to the body to check your drill angle for correctness. If the neck is too long at this point, trim its length until the head rests on top of the collar, as shown here.

Use your knife to remove the sharp edge from the right side of the body, from about the waist up to the shoulders. (To get an idea where we are headed, imagine that you are holding a saxophone. Look down at the relative angle your left and right arms make with your body).

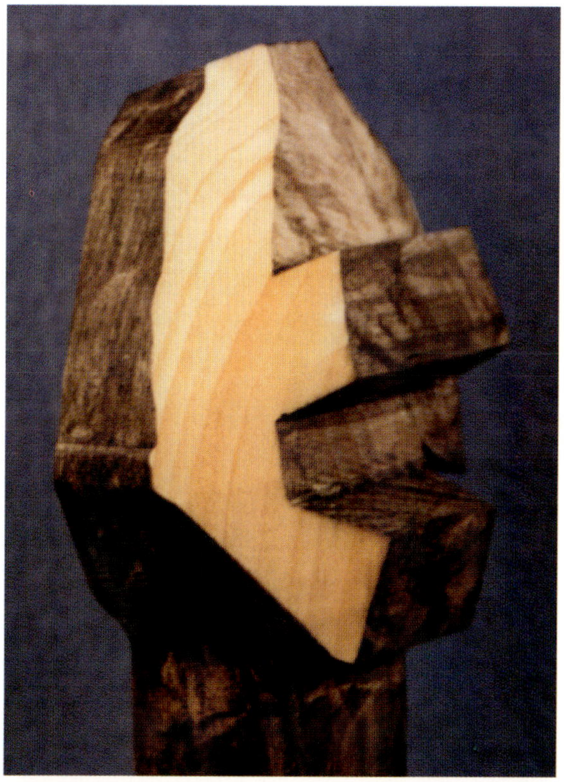

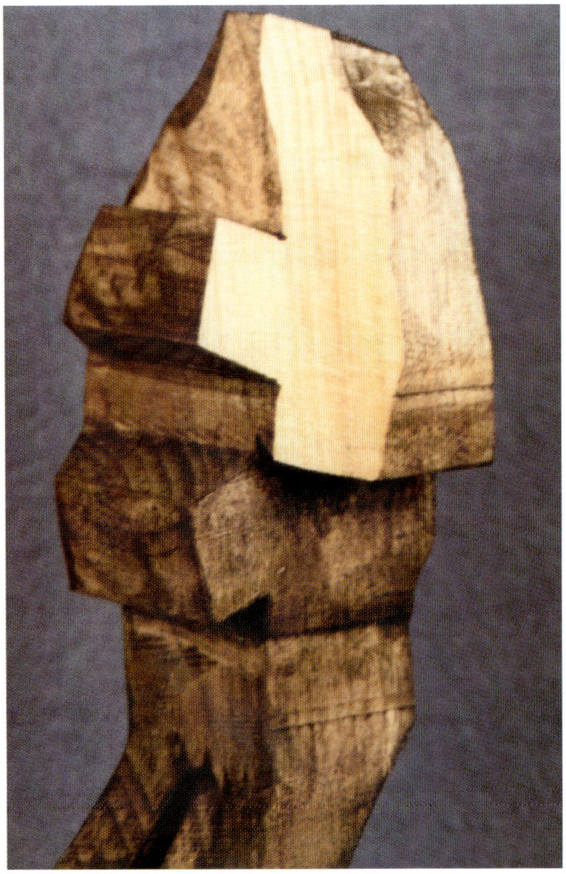

Repeat this process for the left side of the body.

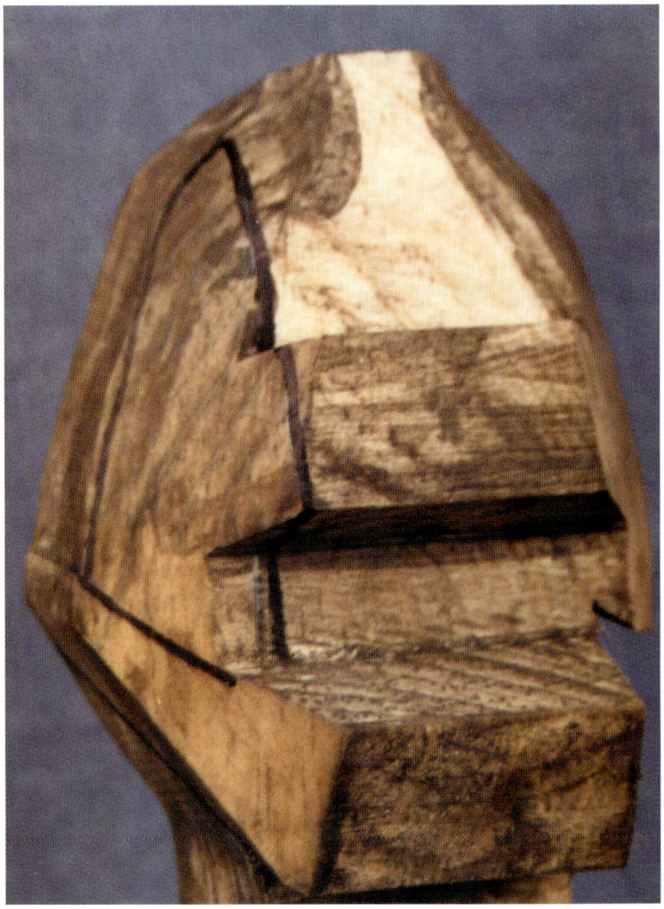

And in the front.

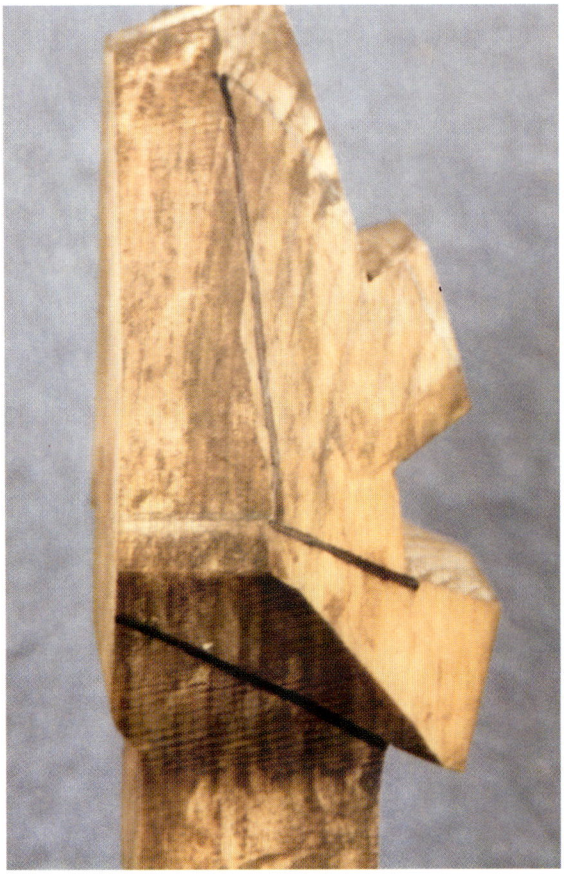

Referring to the pattern and photo, sketch lines to define the right arm on the side...

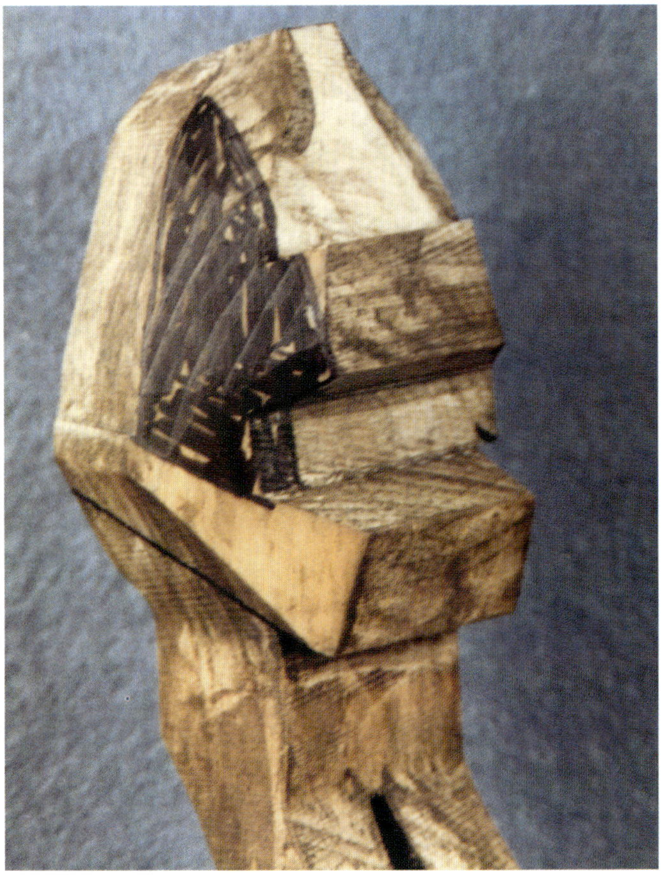

Use your knife and 1/4" straight gouge to remove the darkened area of wood...

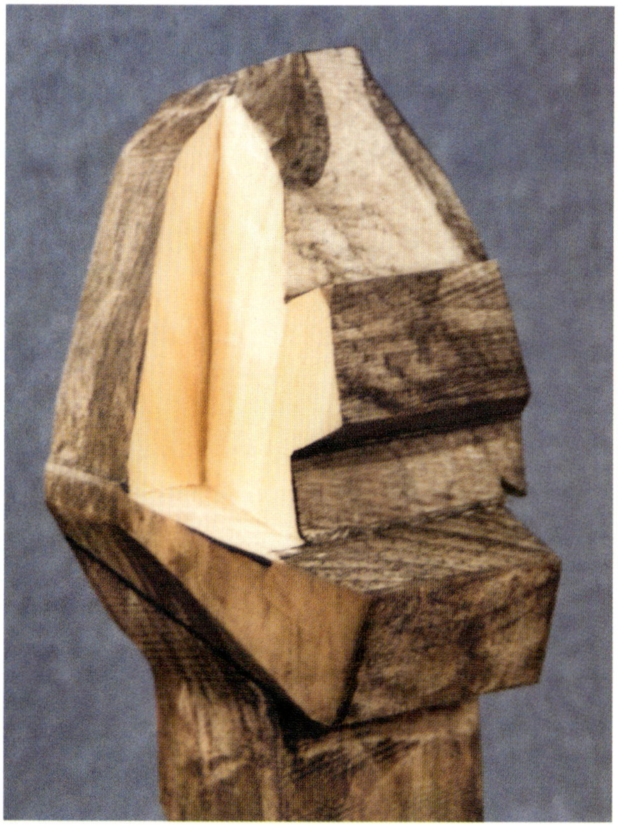

As seen here. Remove small layers at a time. Don't try to gouge away the entire chunk at once.

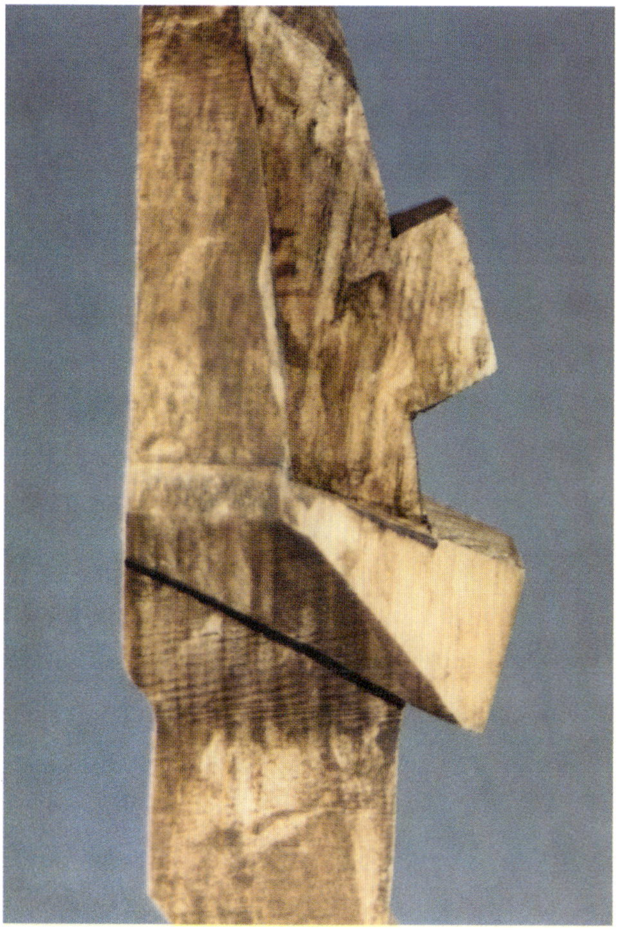

Sketch a line to define the bottom of the right arm.

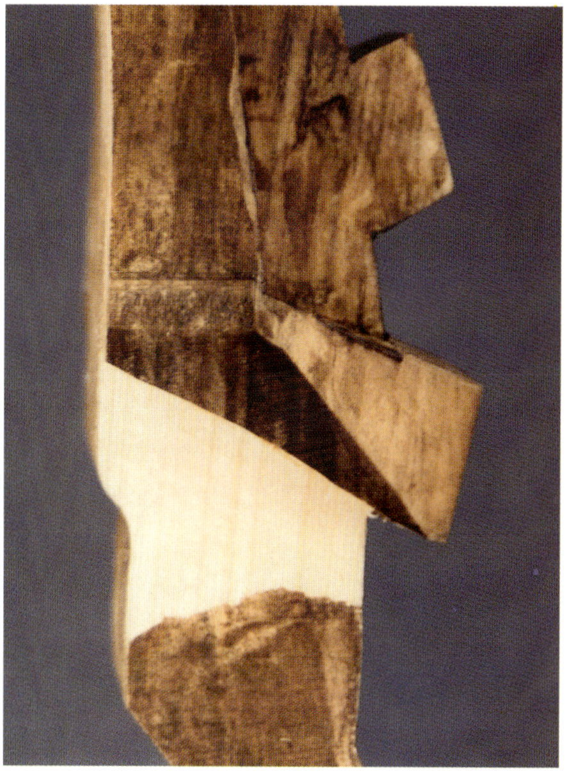

Use your knife and 1/4" straight gouge to remove this wood. The right arm is beginning to take shape.

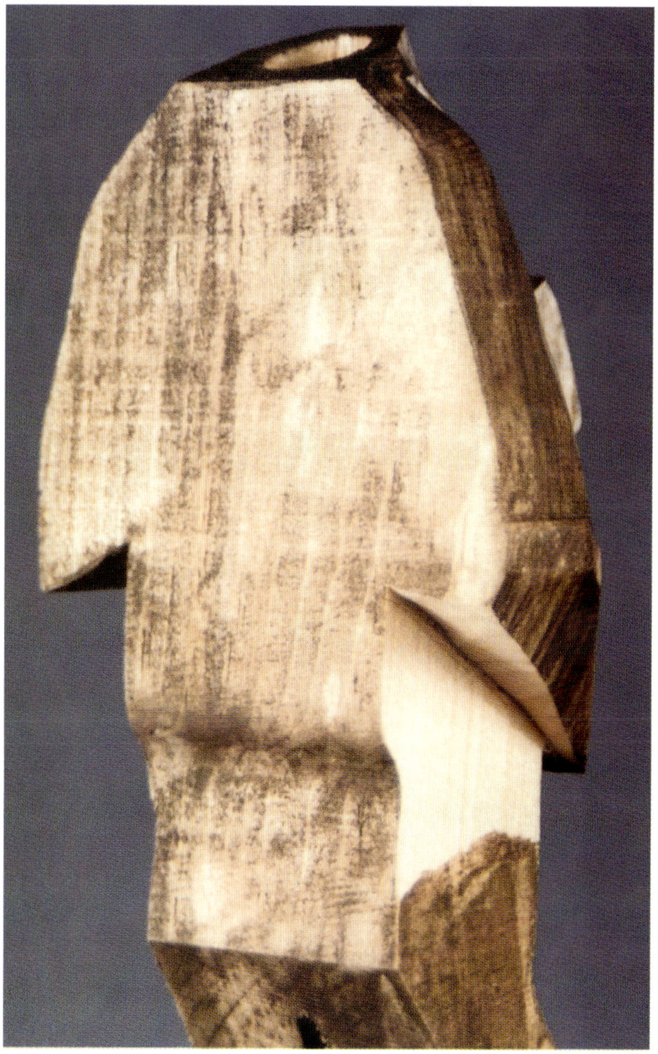

Here is a rear view of the progress so far.

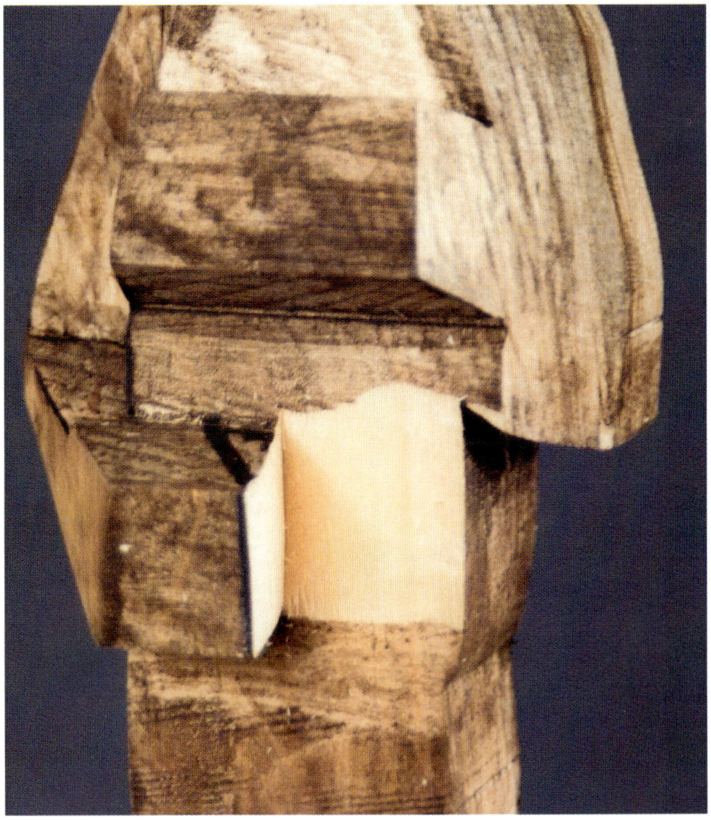

Here is the arm so far, after removing the darkened area using a knife and 1/4" straight gouge.

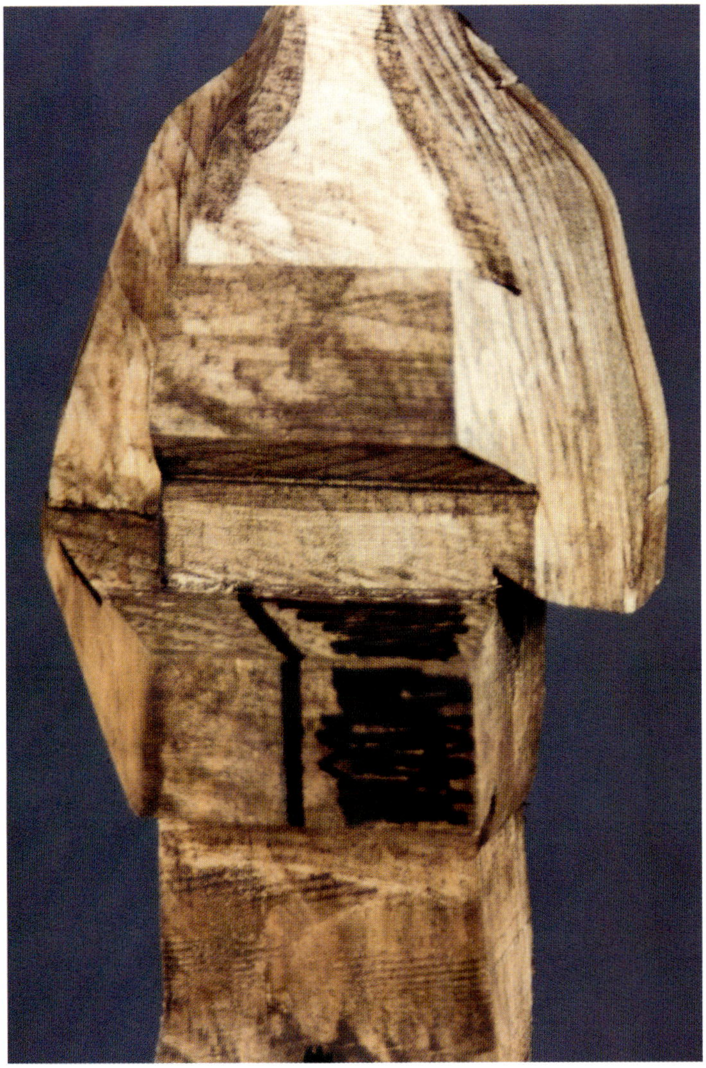

Sketch lines to define the right arm as it comes across the belly, and to set the basic width of the sleeve. We will want to remove the darkened areas to finish roughly defining the arm.

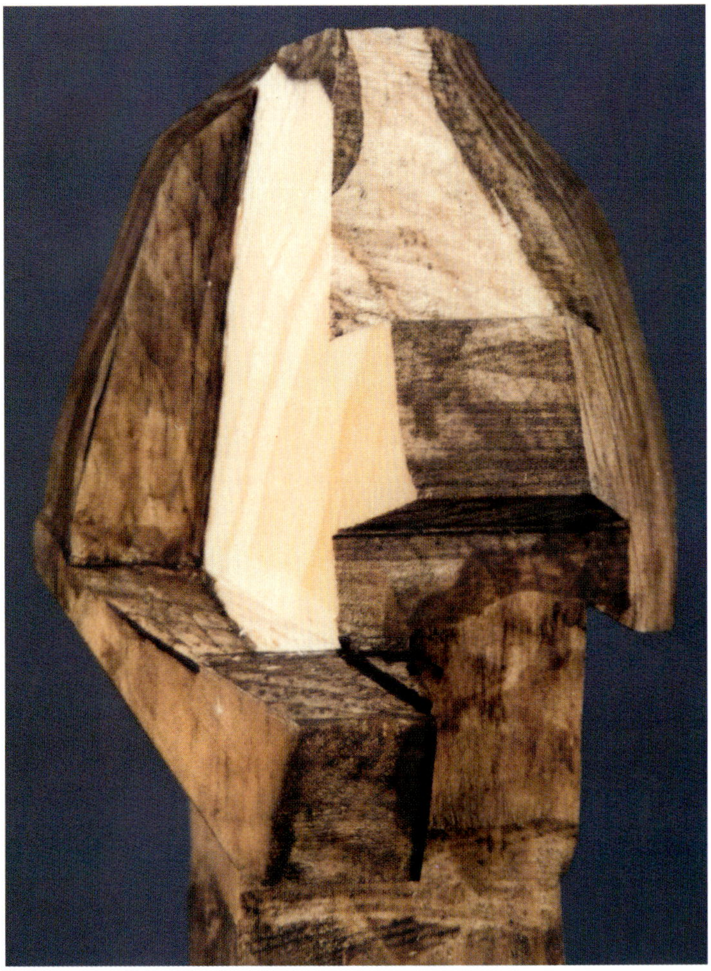

Remove wood from the right side of the chest so the forearm is completely defined.

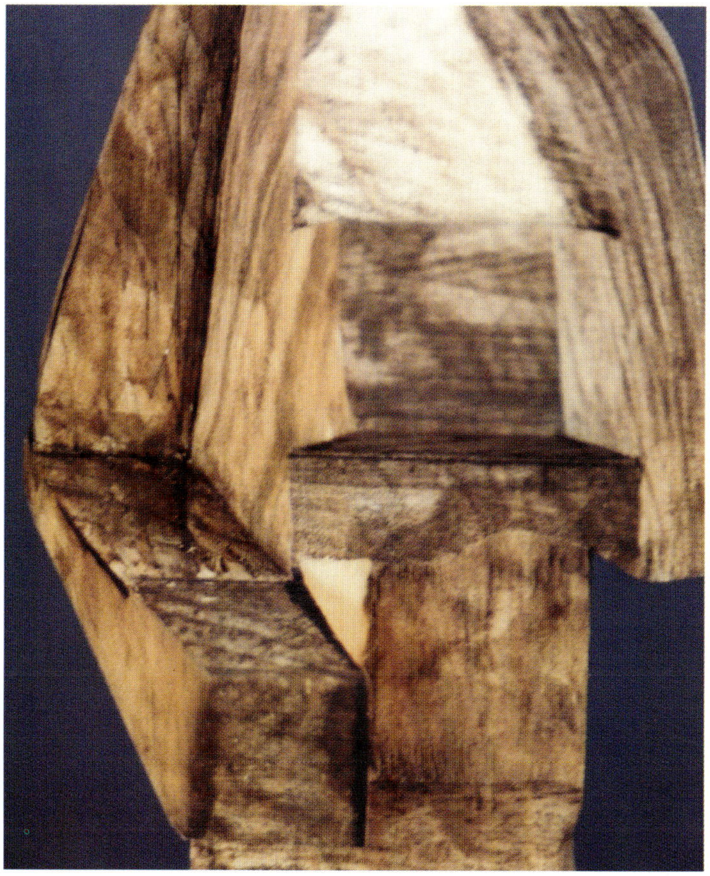

We need to remove the small piece of wood on the inside of the wrist to achieve this shape...

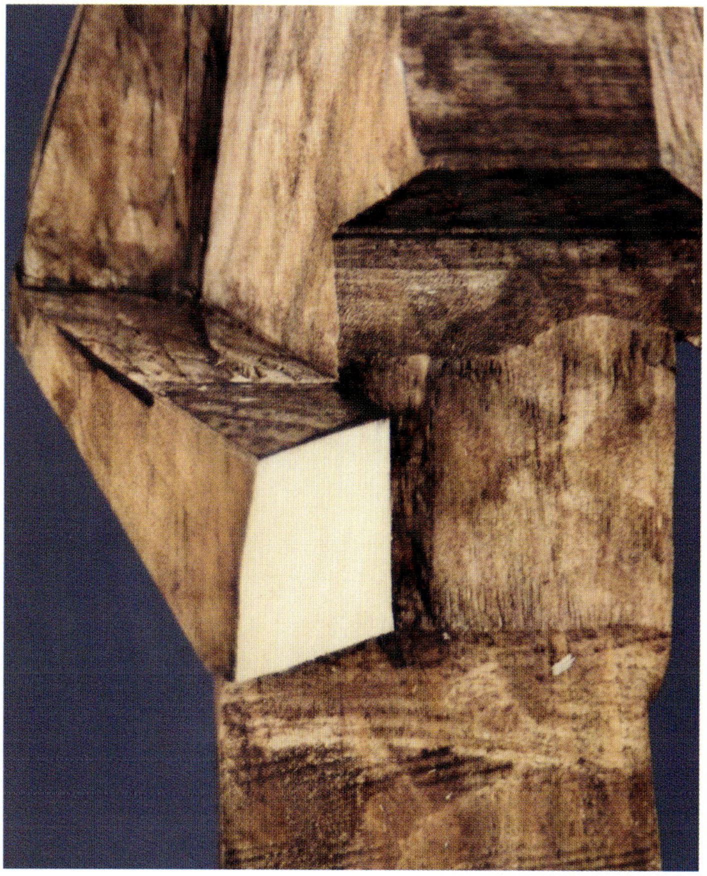

You may have noticed that the end of the wrist is not at the correct angle in relation to the arm. Use your knife to shave away some wood and create a new flat surface that makes a 90° angle with the forearm.

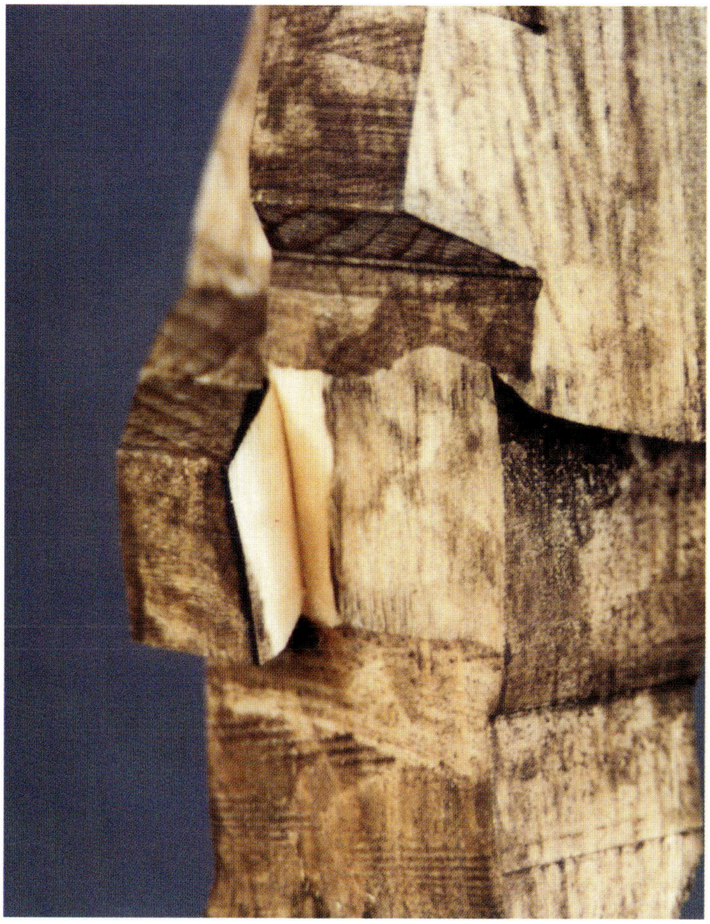

And here's a view from a different angle to show things a little clearer.

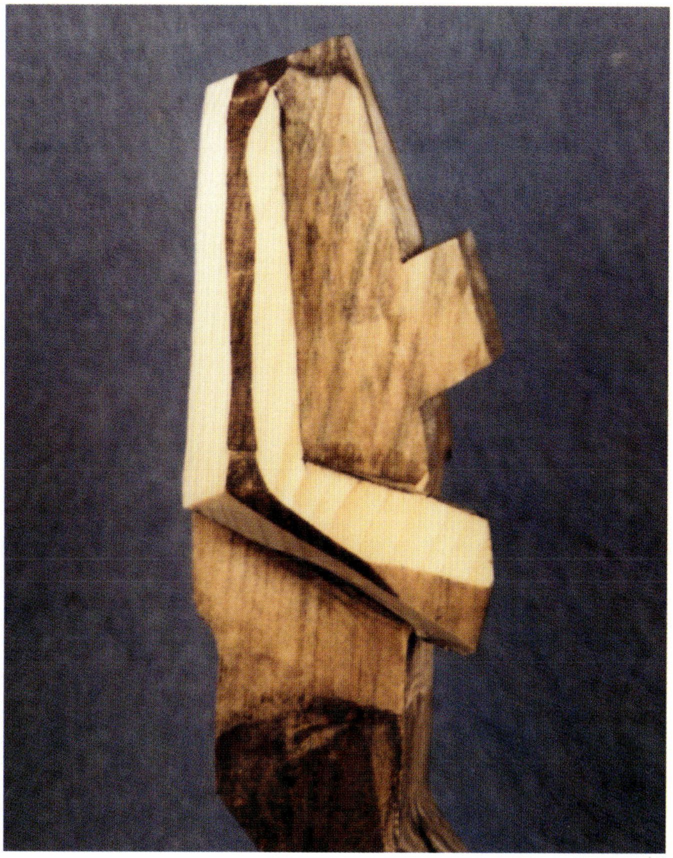

Use your knife to knock off the sharp edges of the right arm to begin rounding it off.

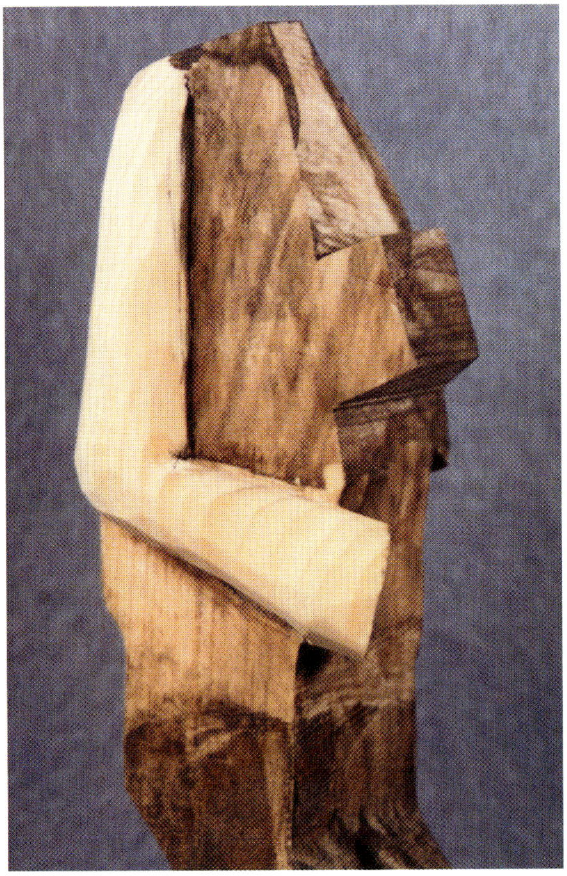

Keep removing the sharp edges until you are satisfied with the roundness of the arm. I like to leave a few small planes and facets so people can see that it is carved...not molded.

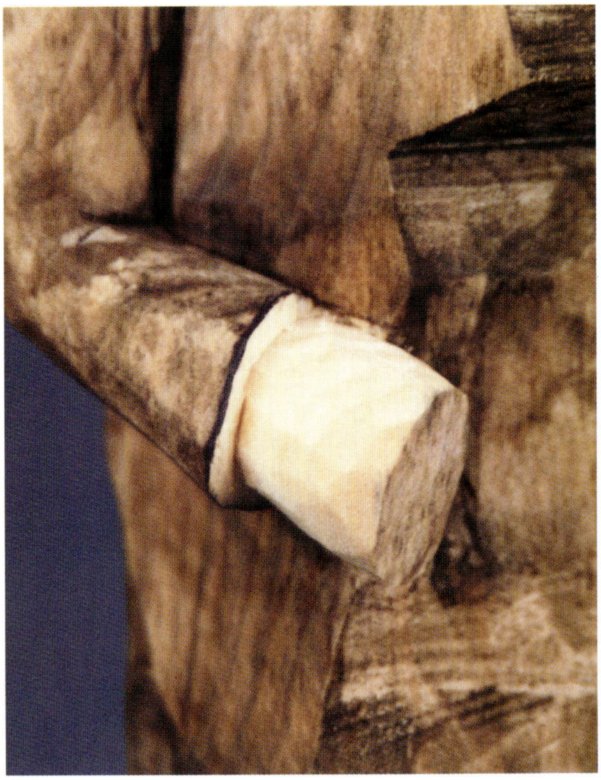

Incise the line about 1/8" deep all around. Then working from the front end of the arm back toward the incised line, remove the wood so the cuff is slightly lower than the sleeve.

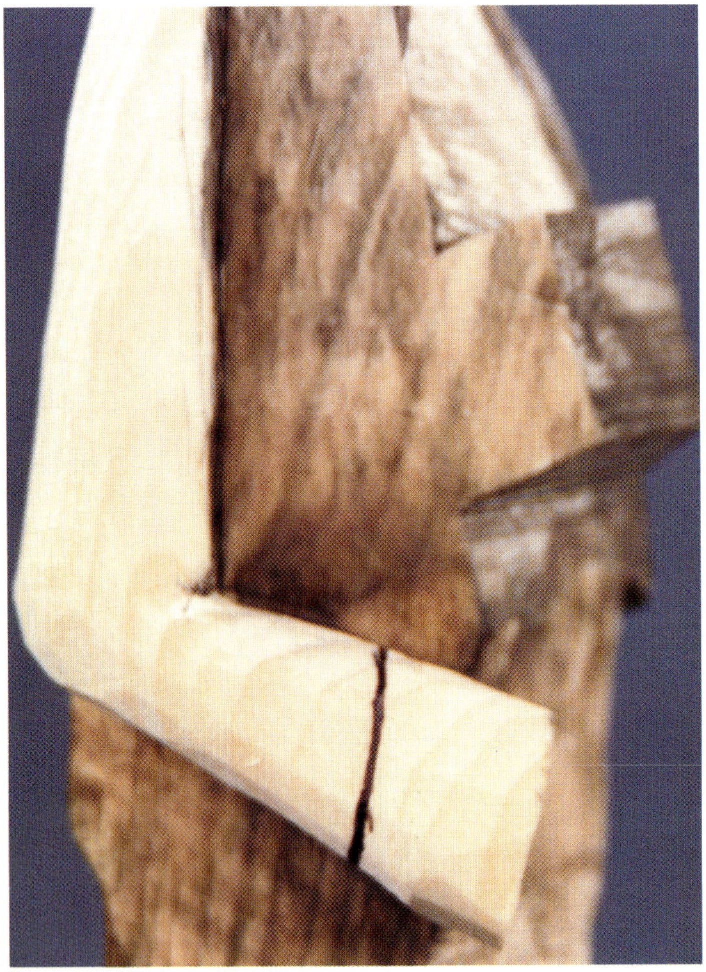

Sketch a line to define the cuff on the sleeve.

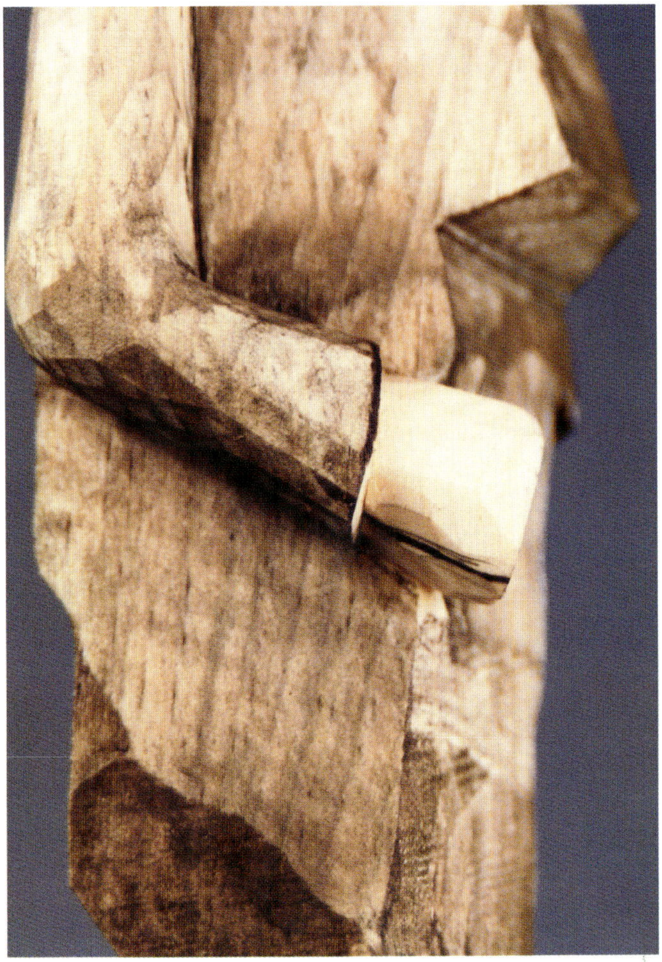

Sketch a line to define the two sections of the cuff.

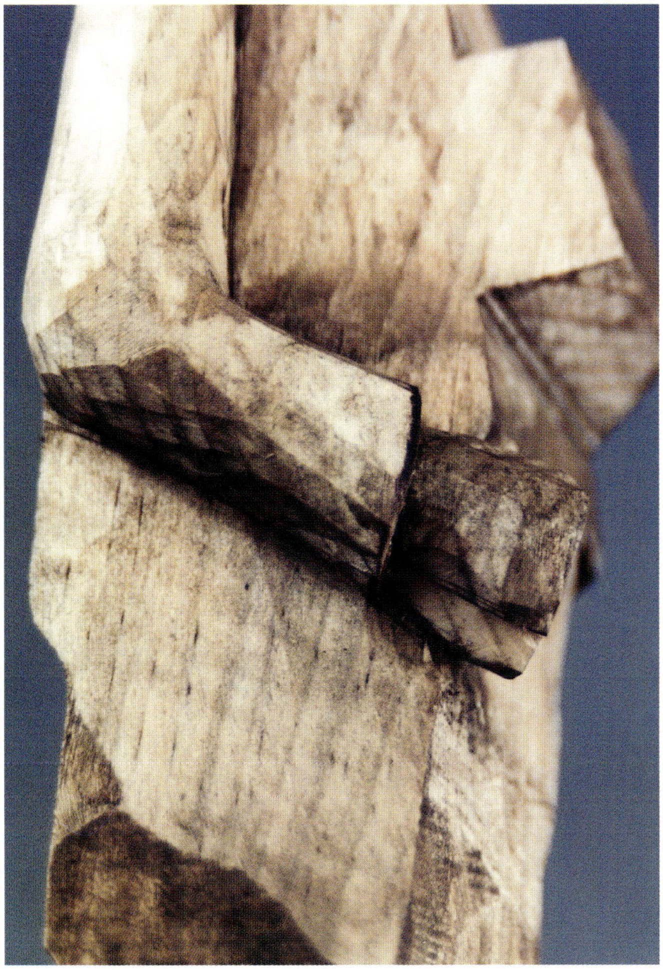

Incise the line lightly, then remove a small amount of wood from the lower section.

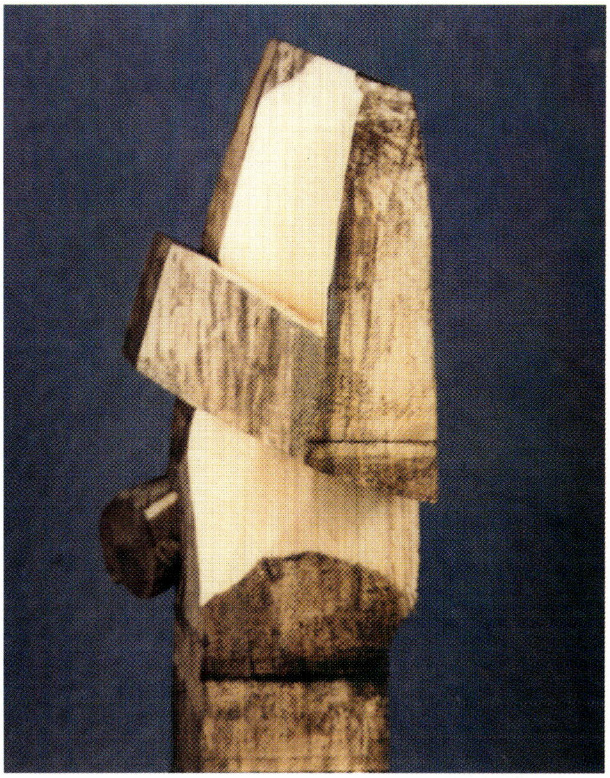

For the left arm, repeat the procedure you just used in creating the right arm. First remove the wood above and below the arm...

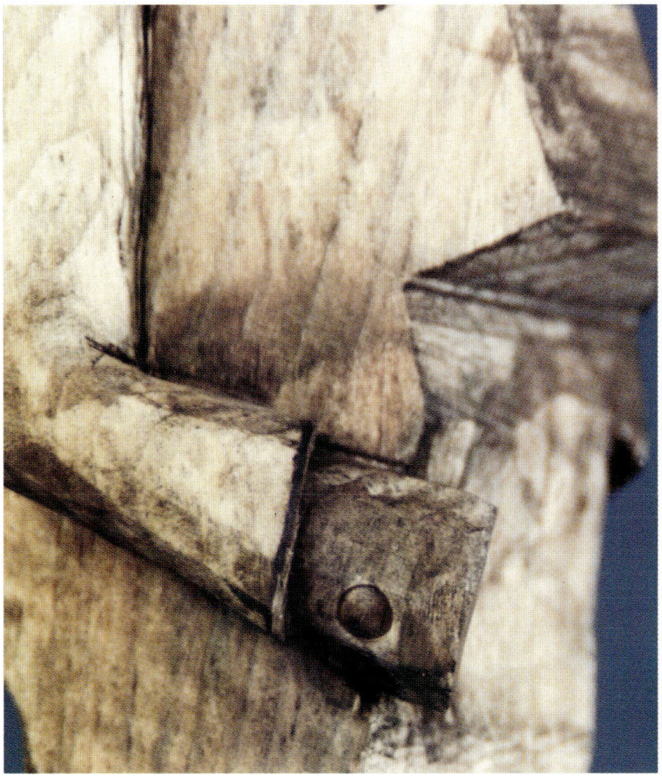

Use a 3/16" eye punch to put a button on the upper part of the cuff.

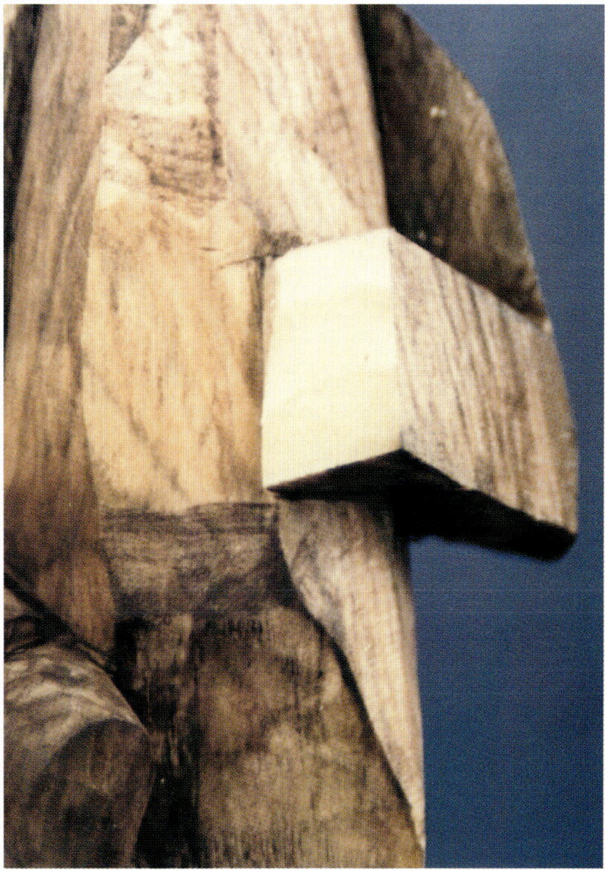

Set the correct angle for the end of the arm...

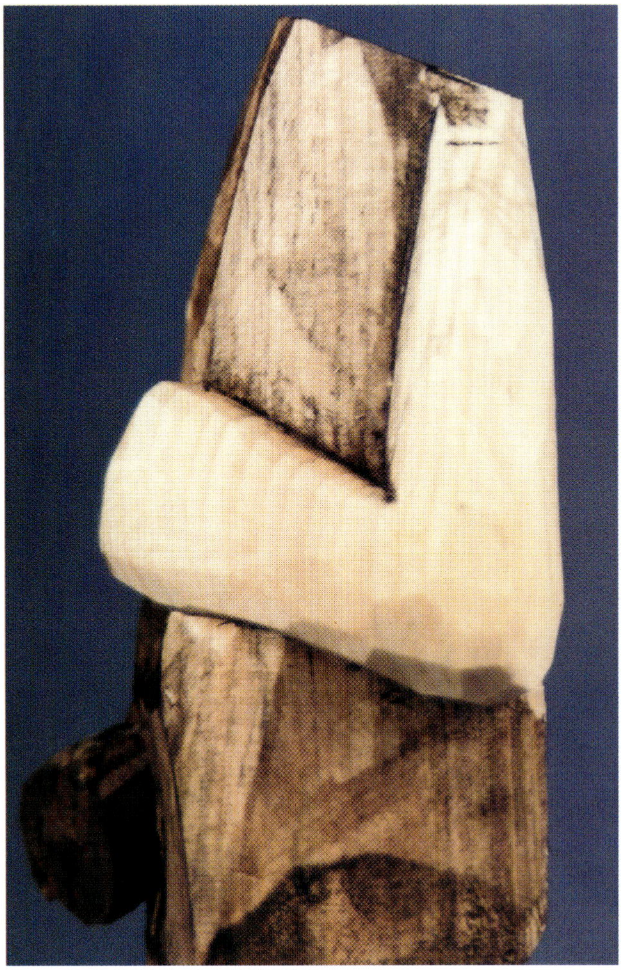

Round off the arm...

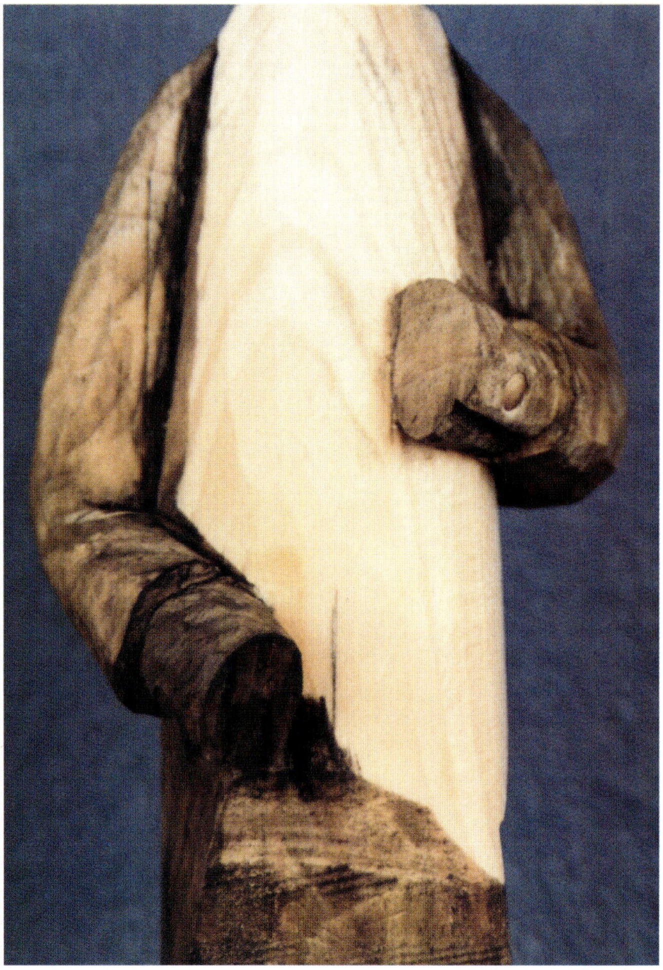

Round off the sharp edges on the chest, above and below the arms. We'll work below the waist shortly.

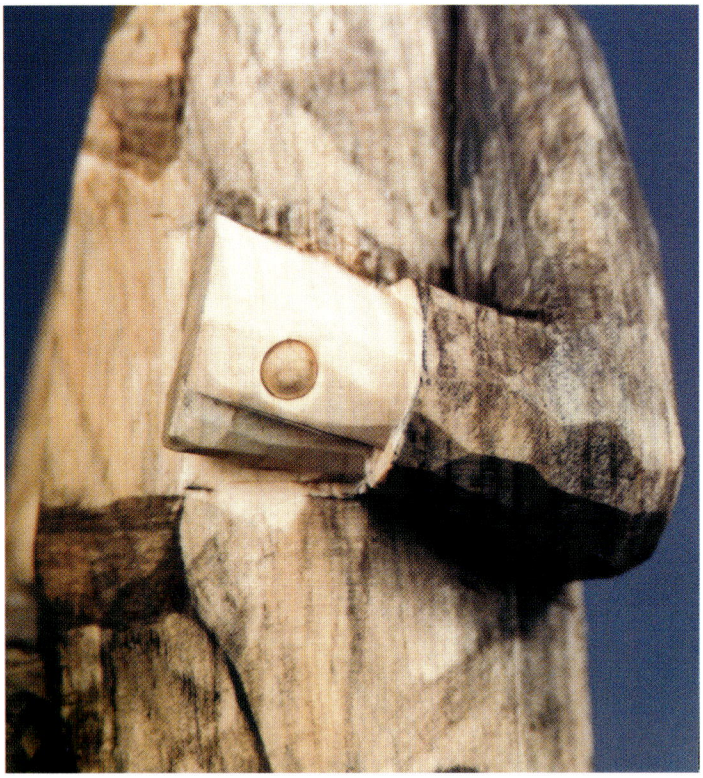

And make the cuff and button.

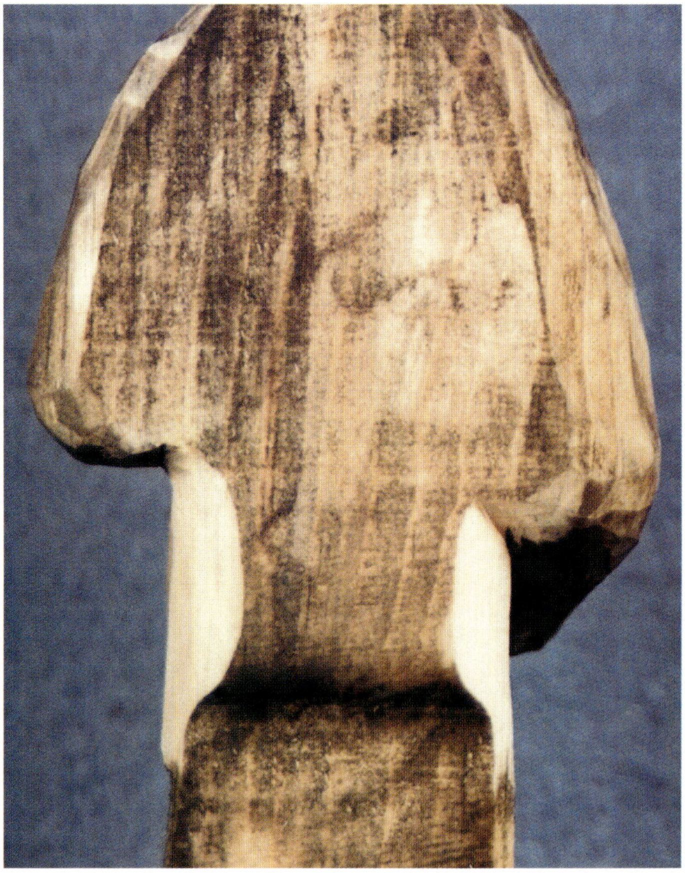

Round off the sharp edges in back, from the waist up.

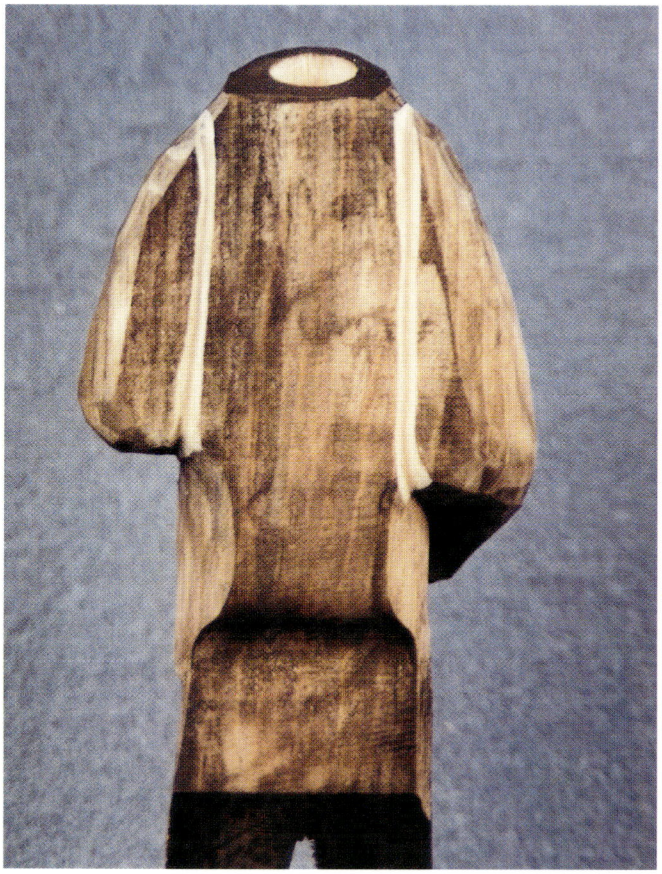

Use a 1/4" "V" gouge to define the arm separation from the body in the rear, and round off the sharp edges with your knife.

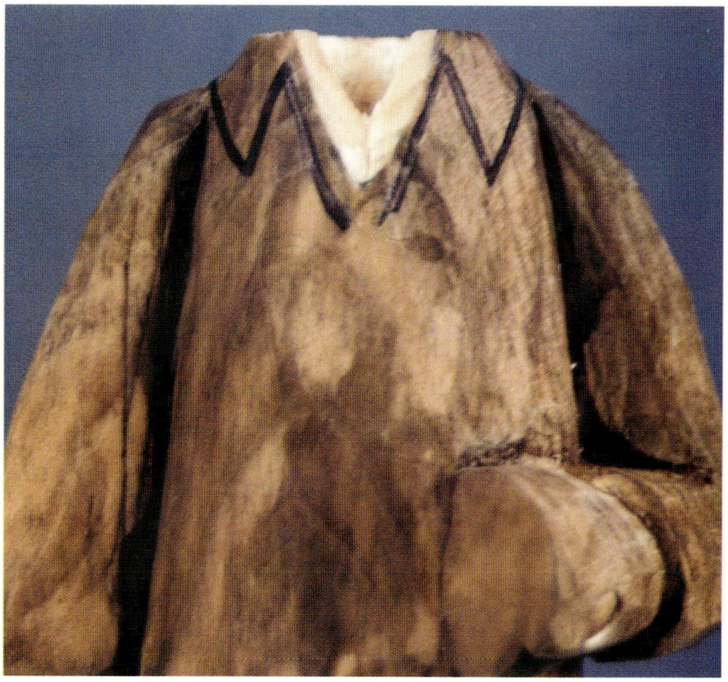

Next, sketch in the collar ears on the left and right sides...

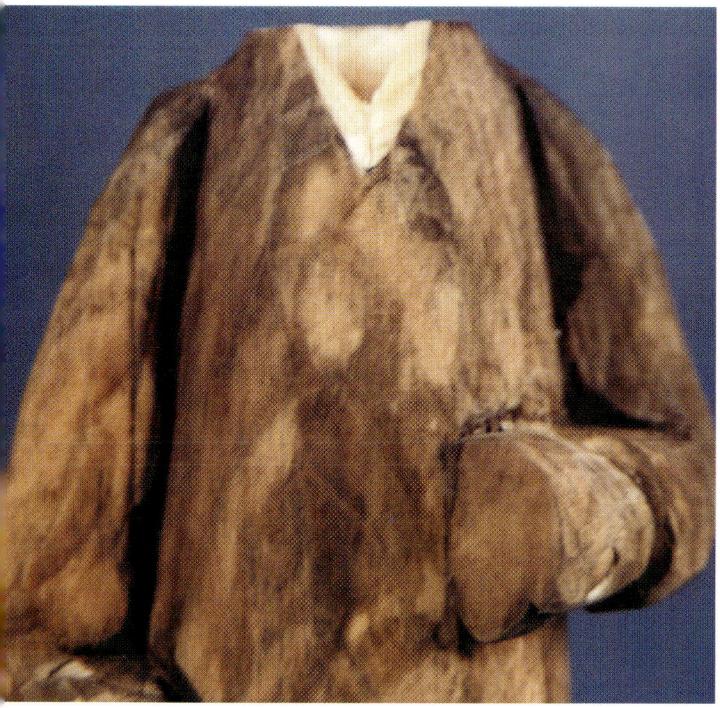

To start the collar, remove a "v"-shaped section of wood, about 1/2" down from the top of the collar, using your knife tip.

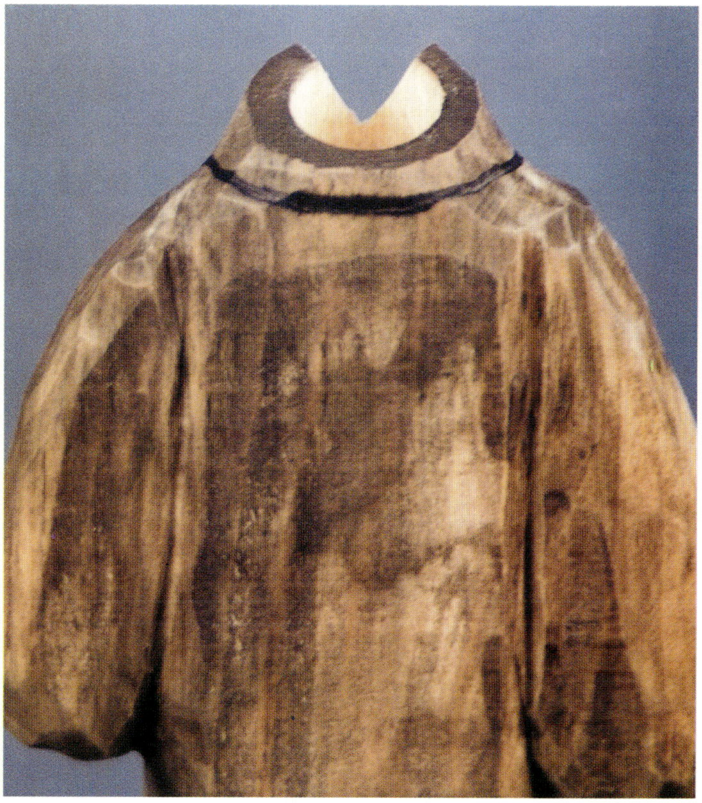

And around the rear of the neck.

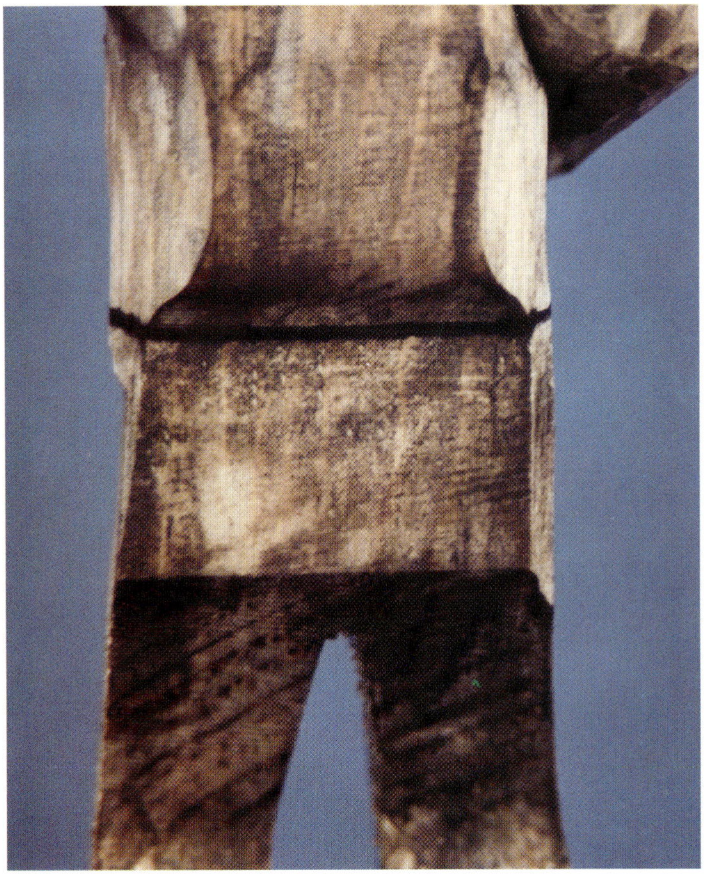

Sketch the waist in the back.

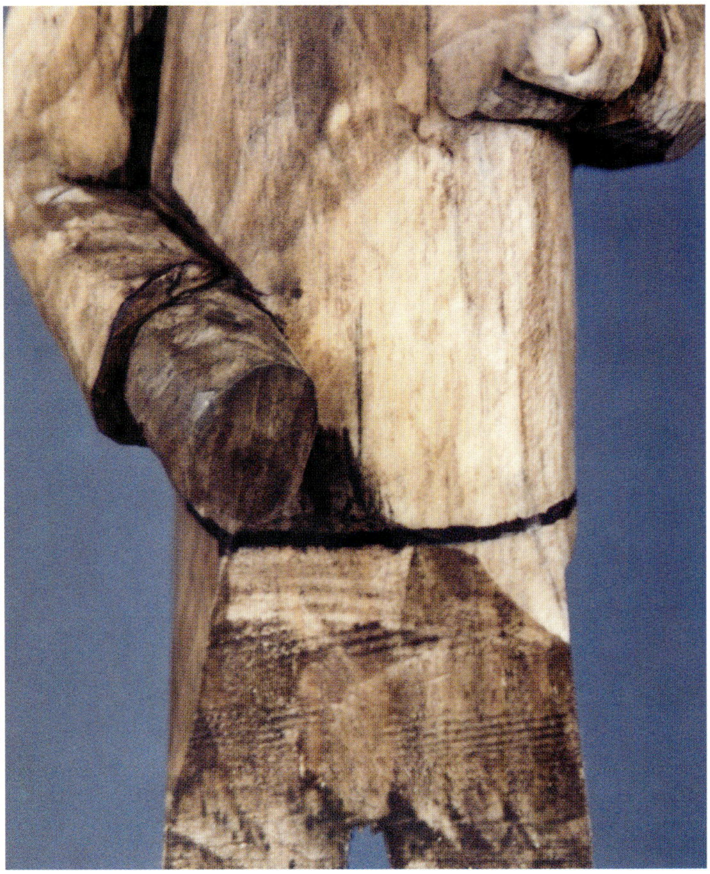

Across the front...

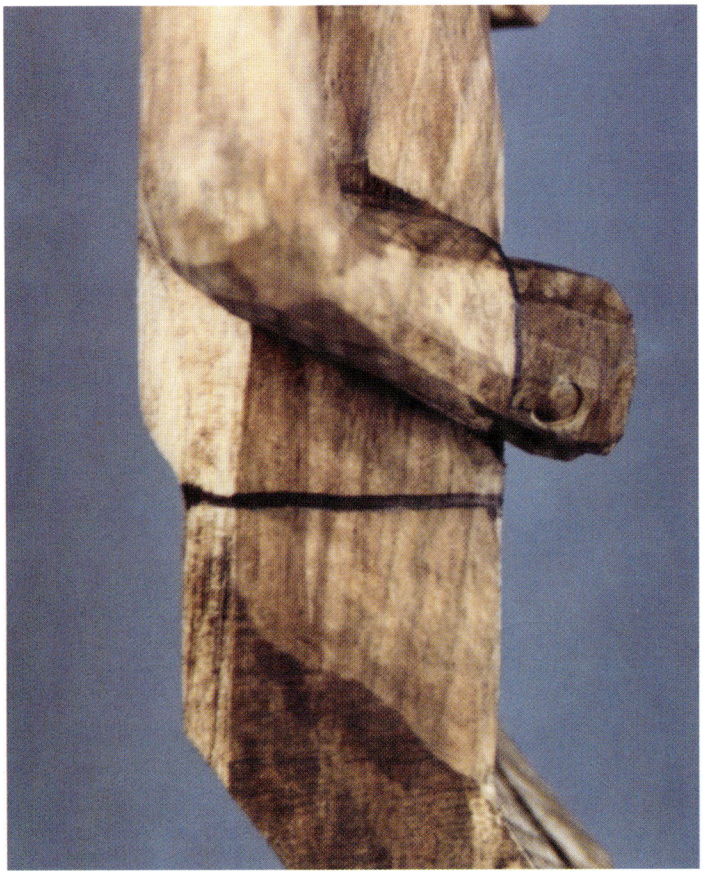

Around the right side...

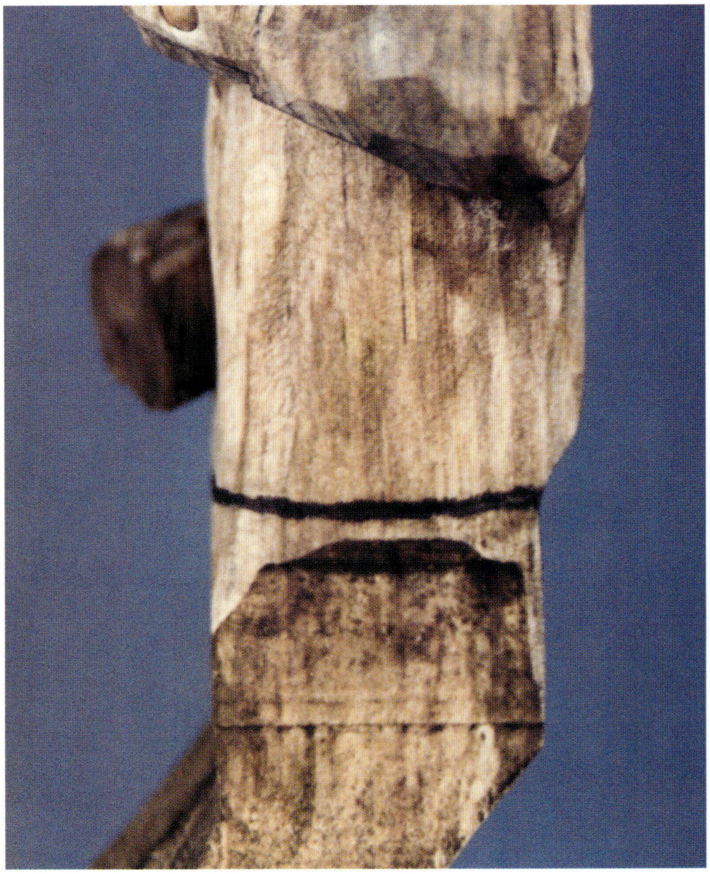

And around the left side.

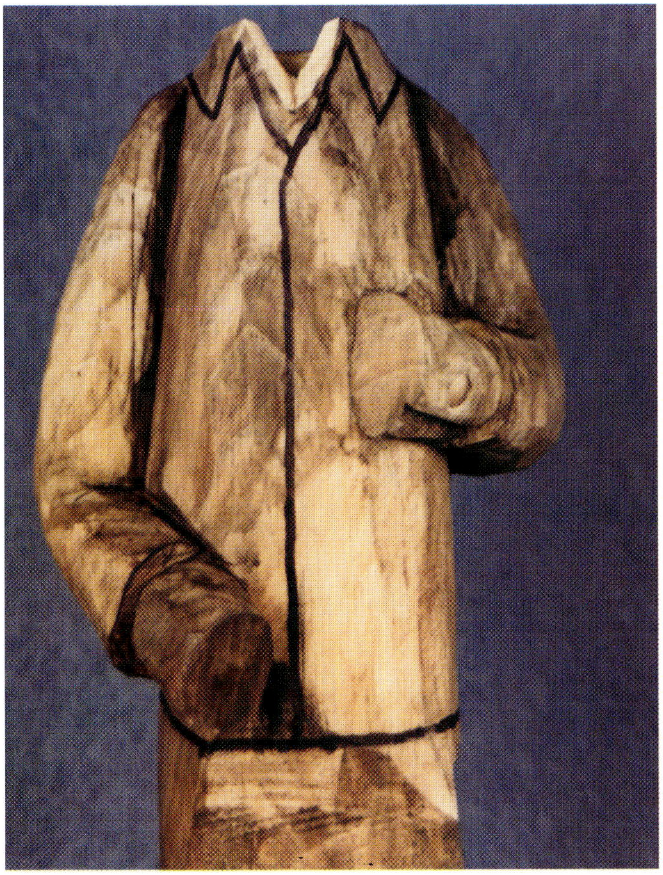

Now that we have defined the collar and waist, we need to create the seam of the shirt down the front. Sketch a line from the left collar ear down to the waist.

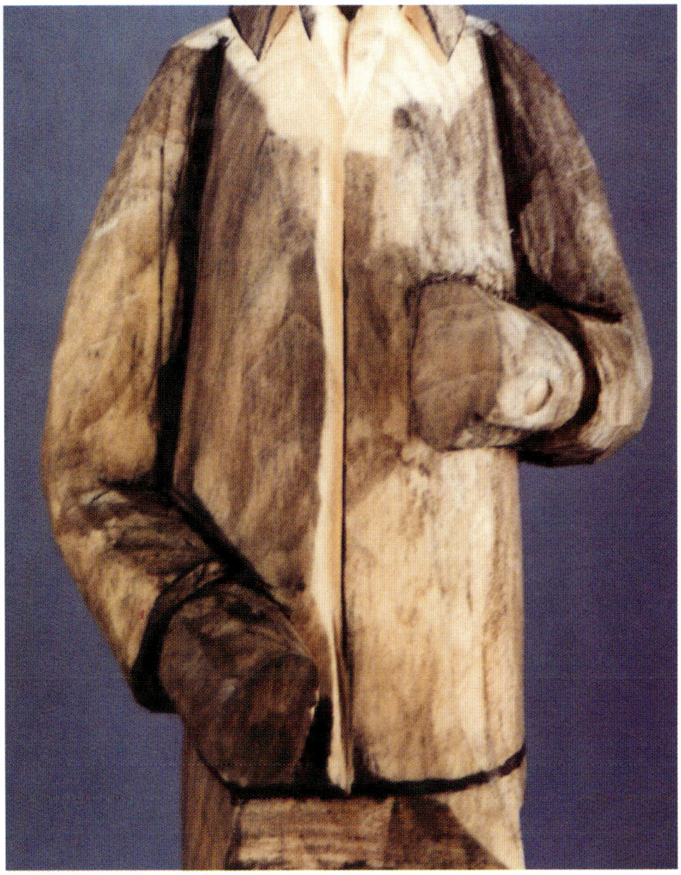

Incise all the collar lines and the seam line about 1/8" deep with your knife. Shave from the shirt toward the incised lines, so that when the wood is removed the collar stands out from the shirt, and the right side of the shirt is lower than the left side. (Guys, look at your own shirt if you are wearing one that buttons down the front. Never hesitate to use yourself as a reference if no one else is around)!

Use a 3/16" eye punch to add a few buttons to the front of the shirt.

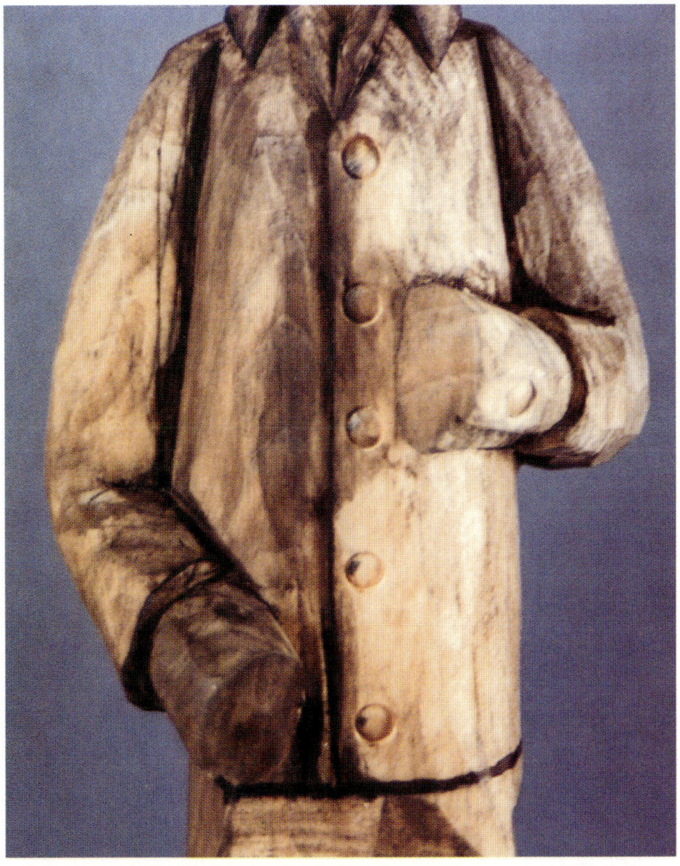

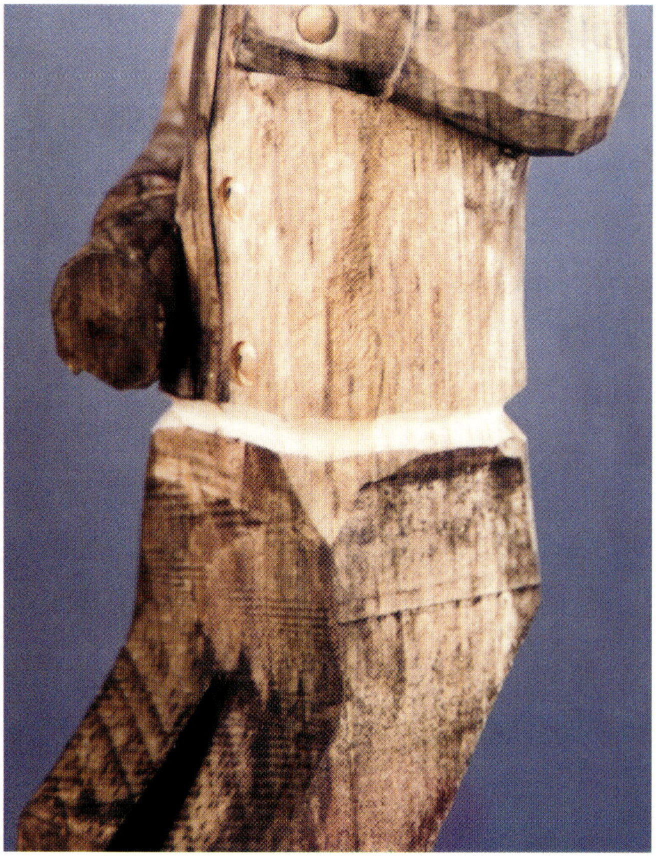

Next, use a 1/4" "V" gouge to follow the line around the waist to define and separate the shirt from the pants.

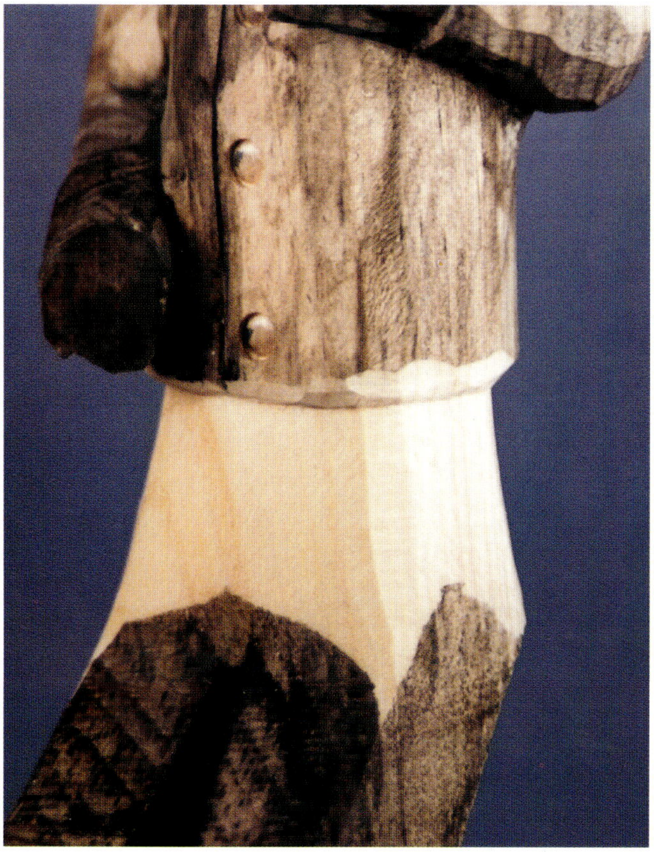

Working from the lower part of the body, shave upward with your knife to remove excess wood from the waist area (on the pants), so the shirt extends out past the pants. This "blousiness" adds to the caricature effect.

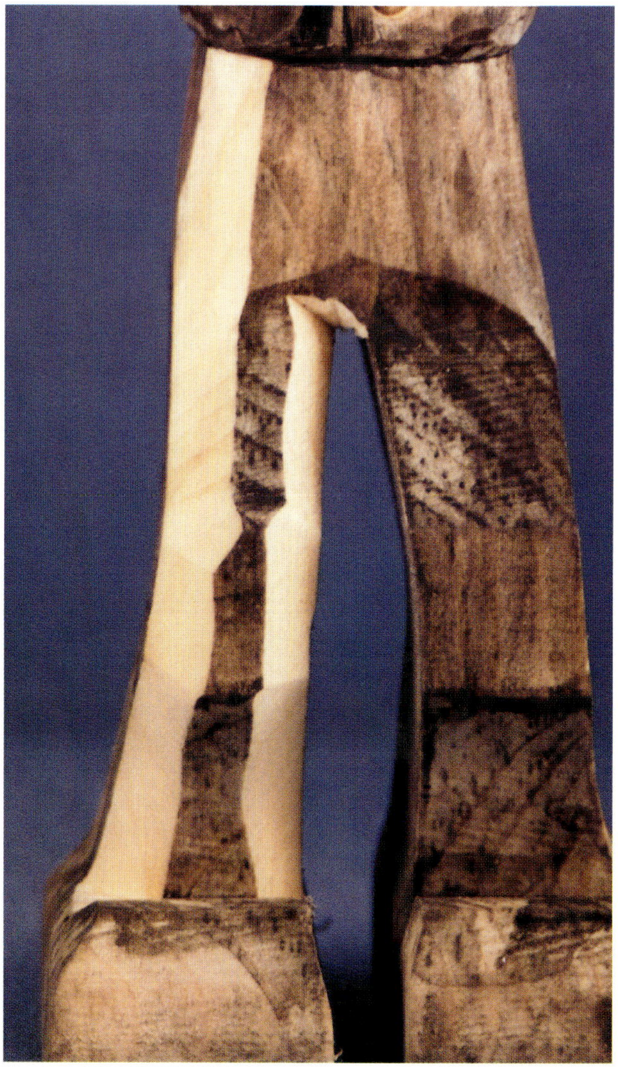

Now, let's work on the legs and feet. I will do the right leg and shoe, and the left leg and shoe will be done using the same procedure. First use your knife to knock off the four sharp edges on the right leg. Work from the waist, all the way down to the shoe area, in front...

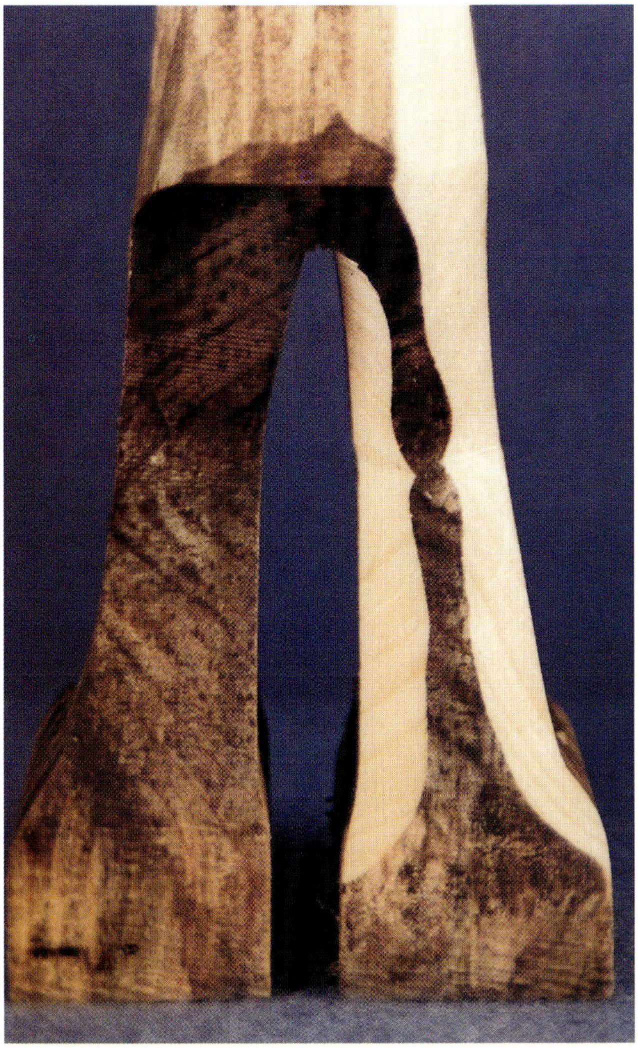

And in the rear.

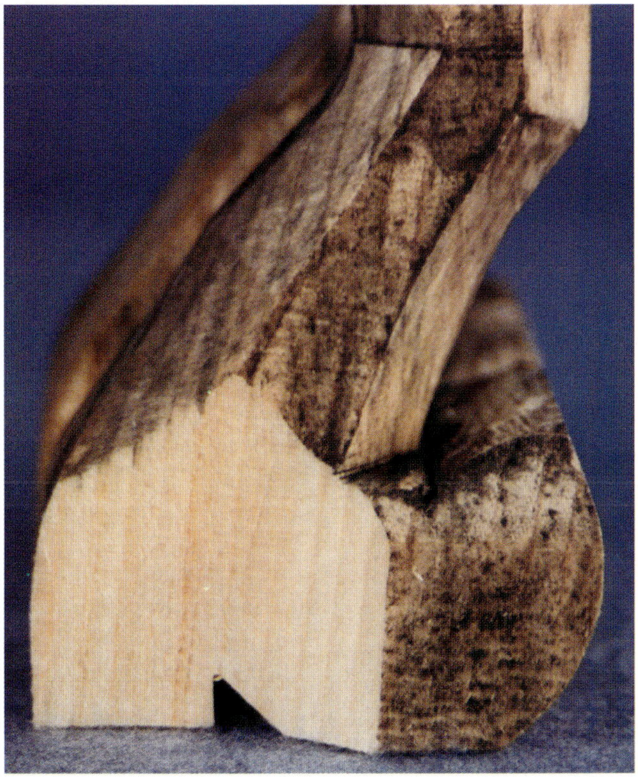

To create a comical flare to the shoe, use your knife to scoop away some wood from the outside section as shown here. This will make the toe area wide in relation to the heel area.

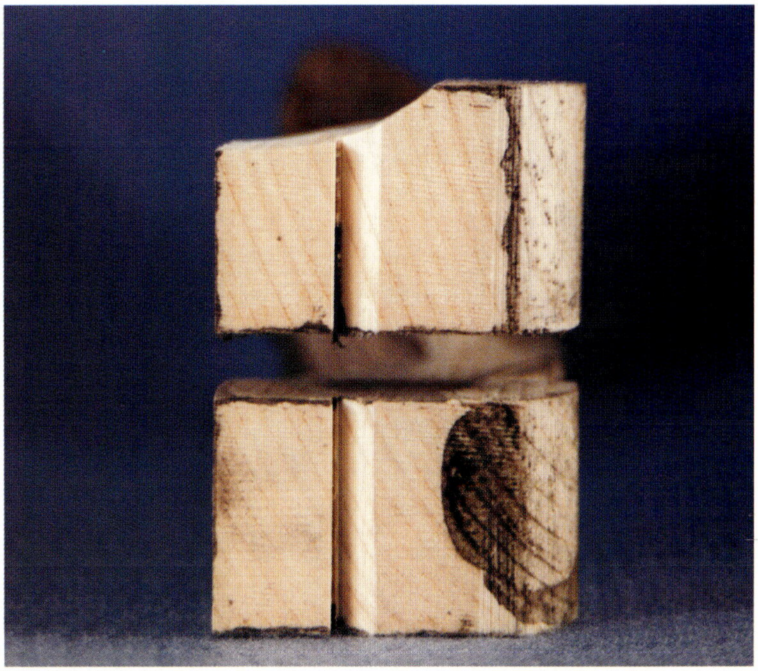

This bottom view of the shoe may help you see the scooped-away area more clearly.

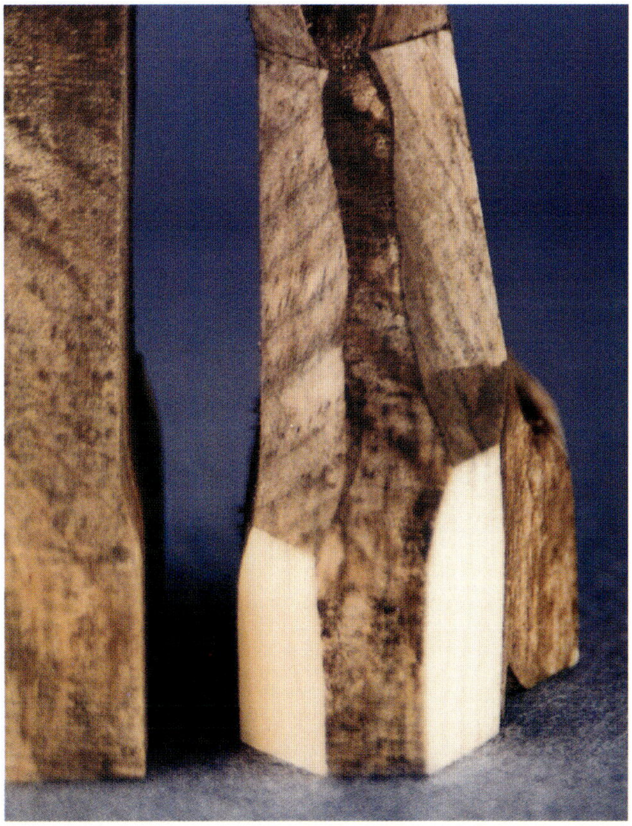

Knock off both sharp edges on the rear of the shoe.

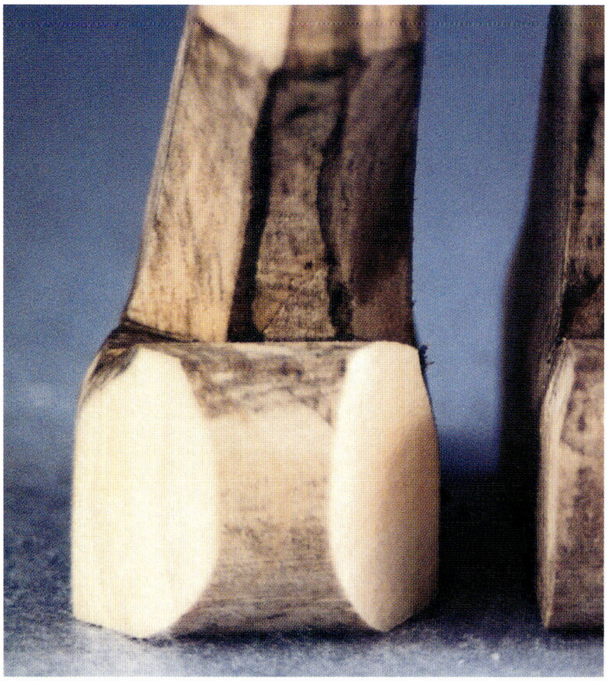

Use your knife to chop off the two sharp edges on the front of the shoe, at about a 45° angle.

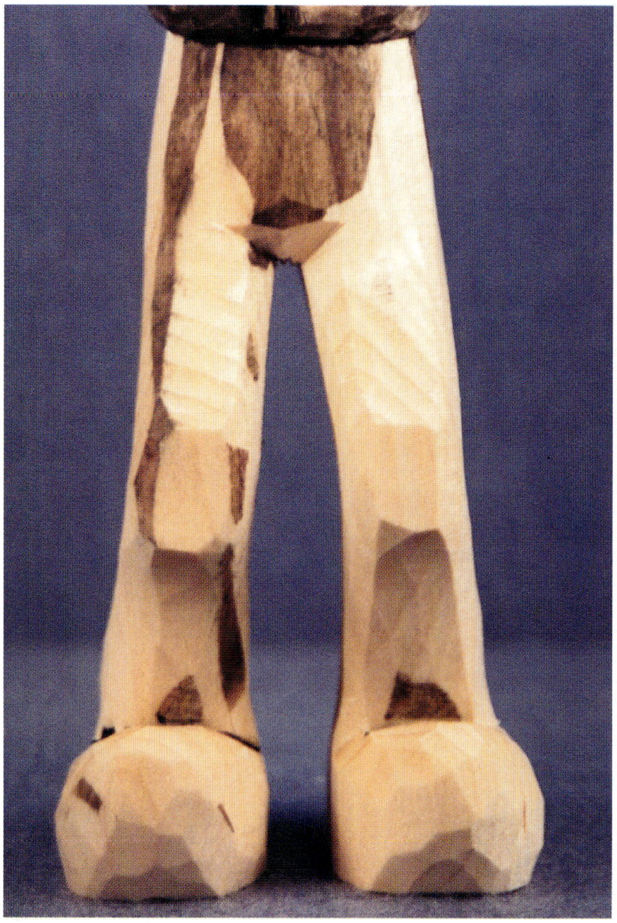

Round off the left leg and shoe using the same procedure as on the right leg.

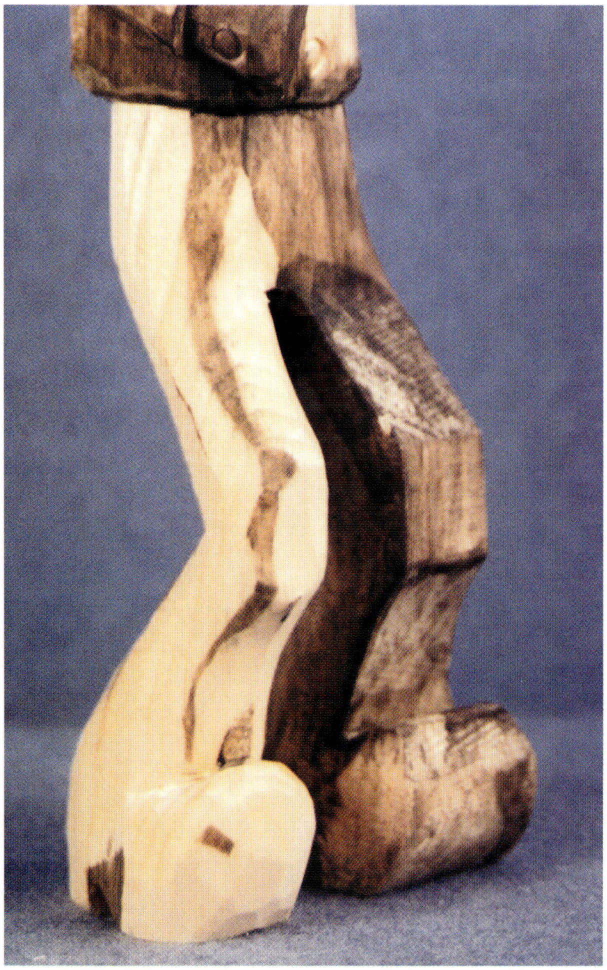

Now, go over the entire leg and shoe, using your knife to remove all the sharp edges.

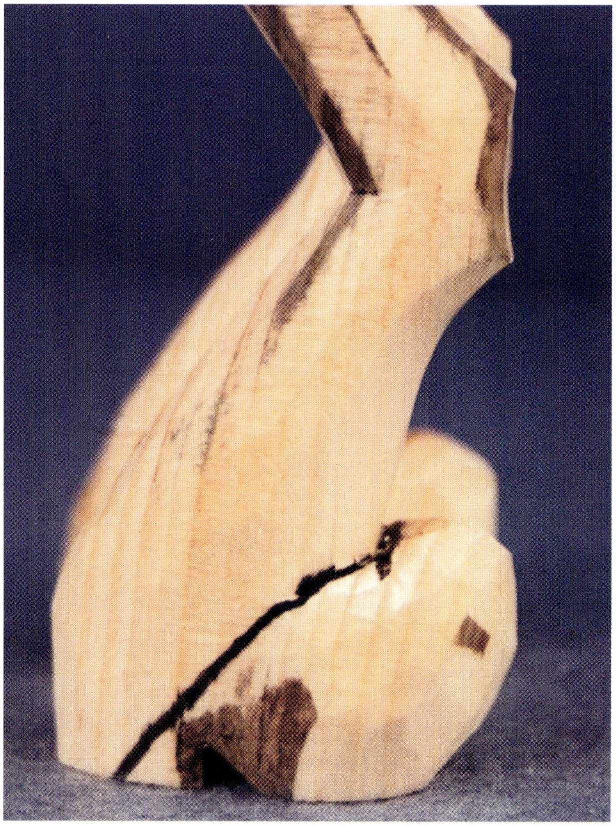

Sketch a line to define the separation between the bottom of the pants, and the shoes.

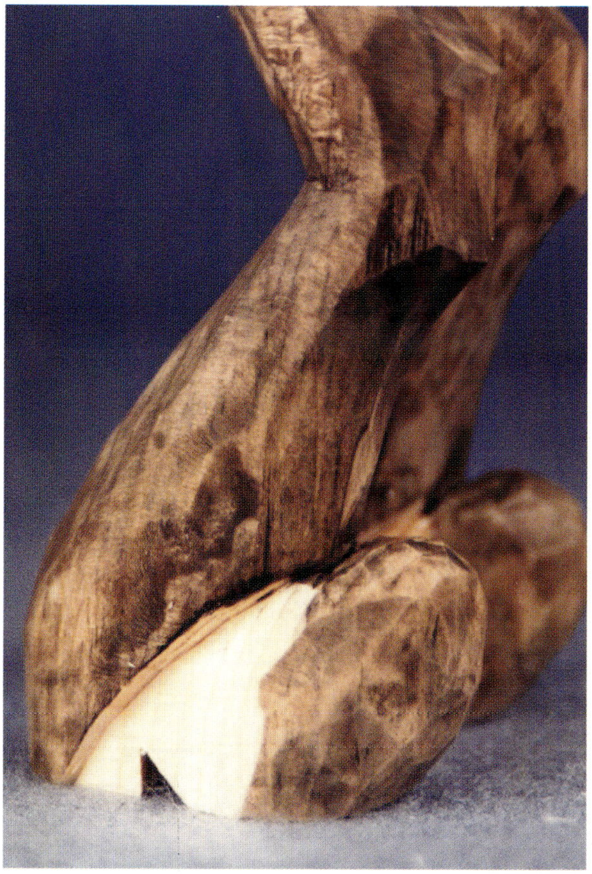

Incise the line about 1/8" deep with your knife. Then shave upward toward the incision so that when the wood is removed, the pants appear to be out over the shoes.

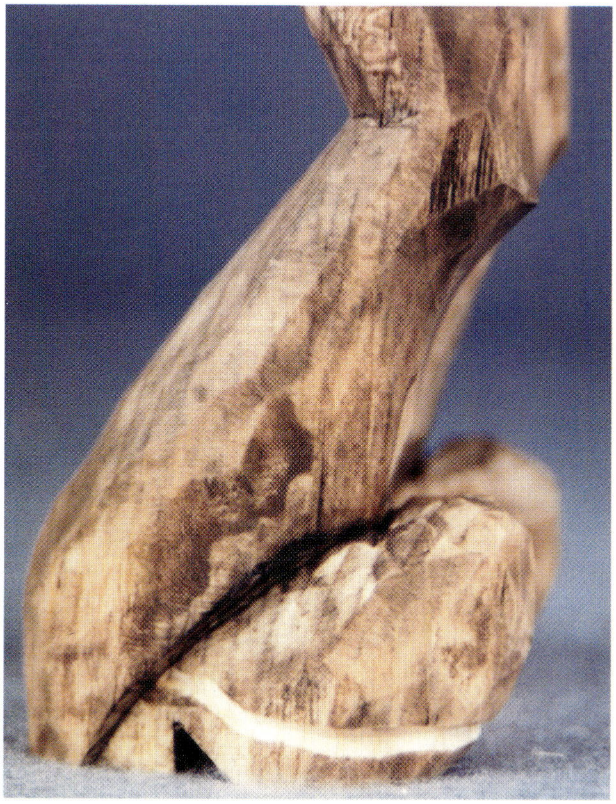

Finish detailing the shoes by using a 1/8" "V" gouge to cut a sole line all the way around the shoes.

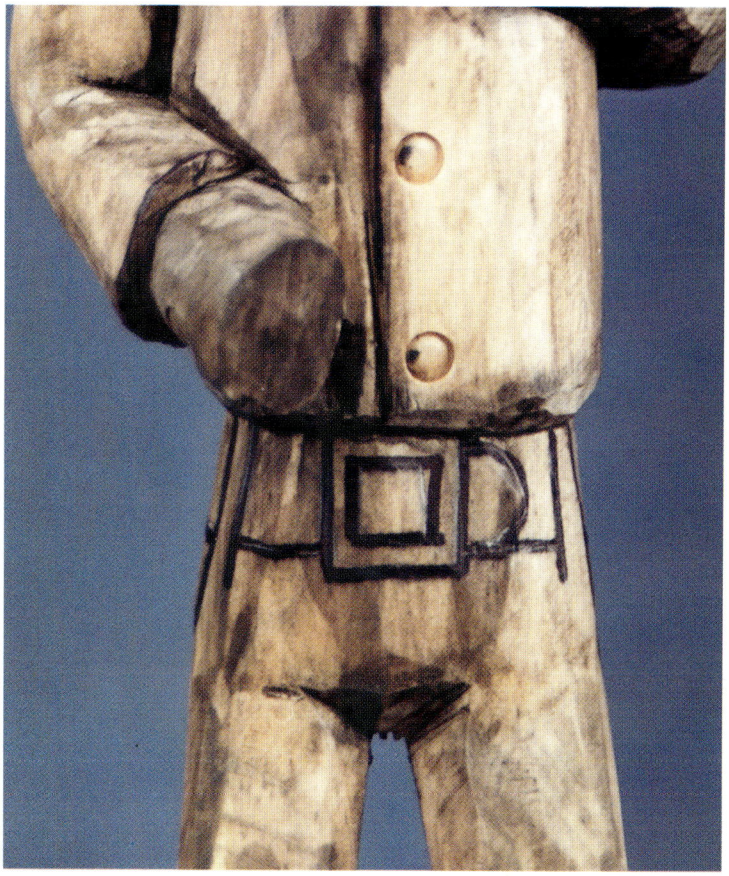

Sketch the belt buckle and belt in front...

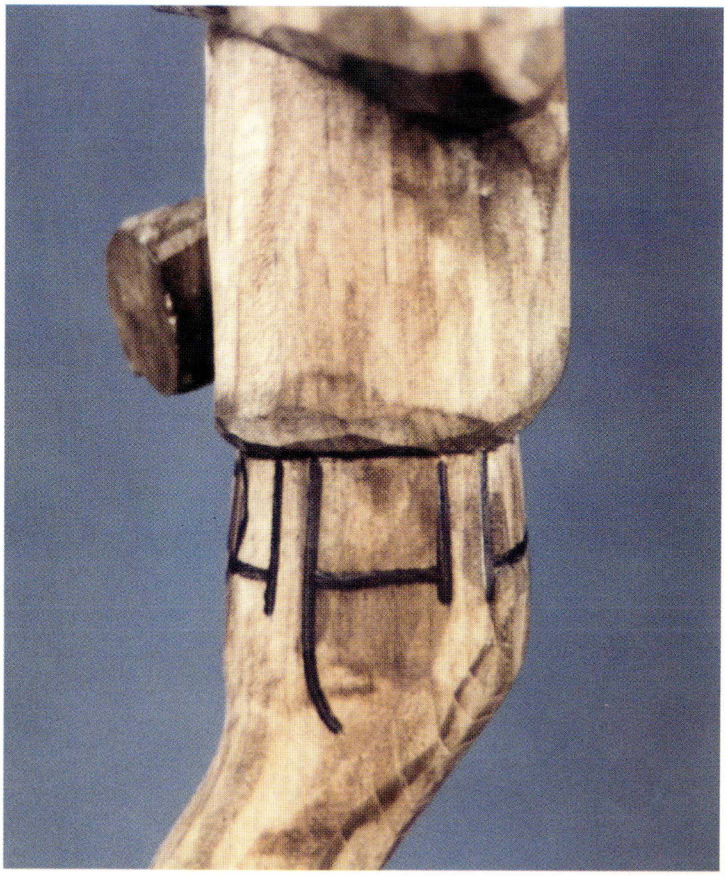

The belt loops, belt and pocket on the left side....

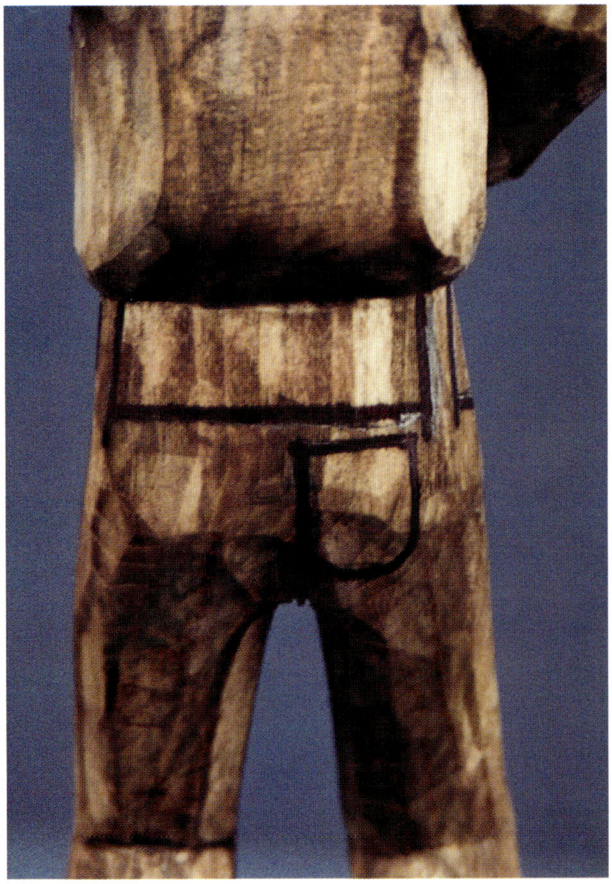

The belt and pocket in the rear...

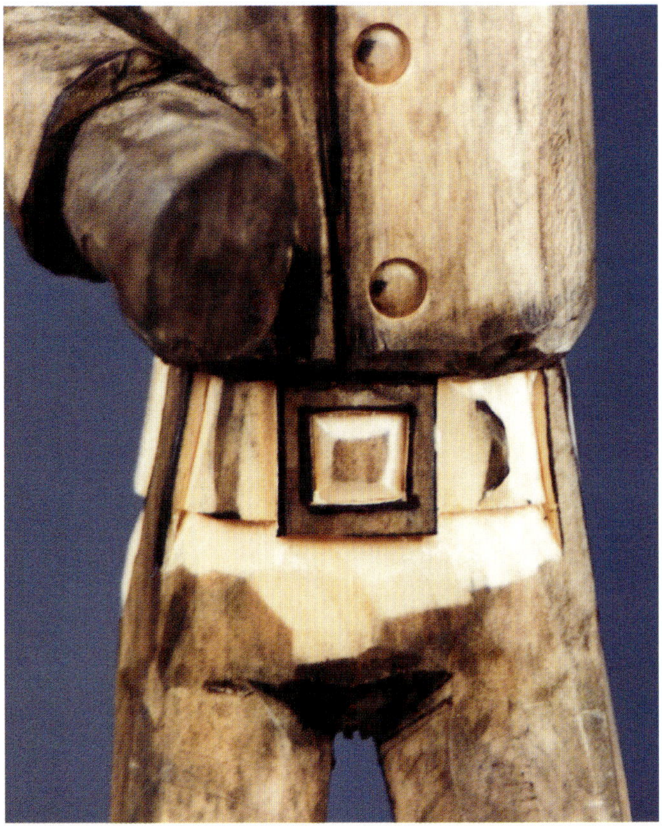

Incise the lines about 1/16" deep. Shave toward all the incised lines so that when wood is removed, the buckle and belt stand out from the pants, and the belt appears to go under the loops.

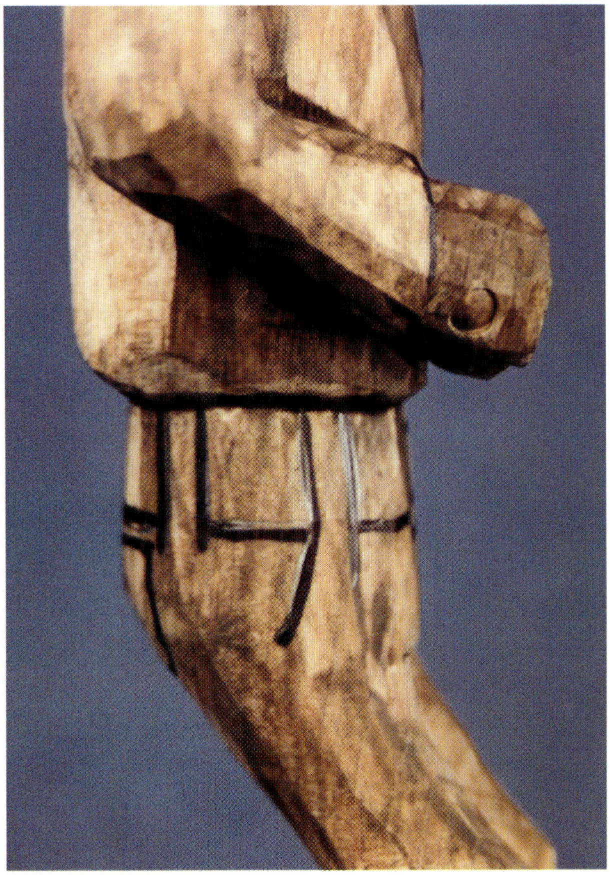

And the belt loops, belt and pocket on the right side.

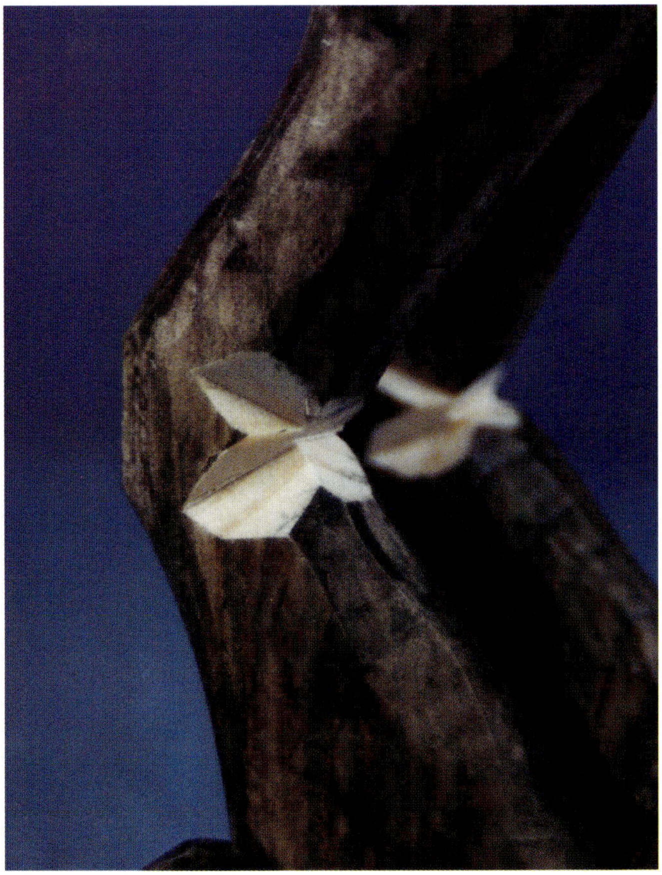

Since the legs are slightly bent, we need some wrinkles behind the knees. Using your knife, remove some "V"-shaped sections of wood to simulate folds in the cloth.

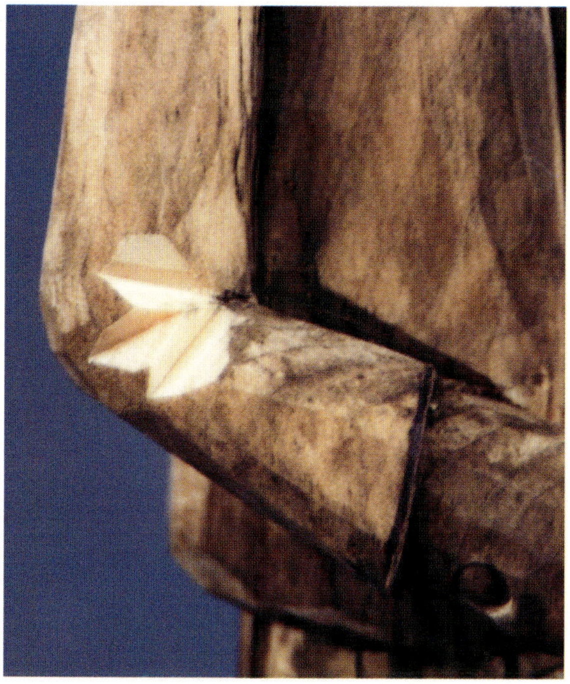

Also, since the arms are bent, we need some wrinkles in the elbow area. Cut some "V" shapes here as you did behind the knees.

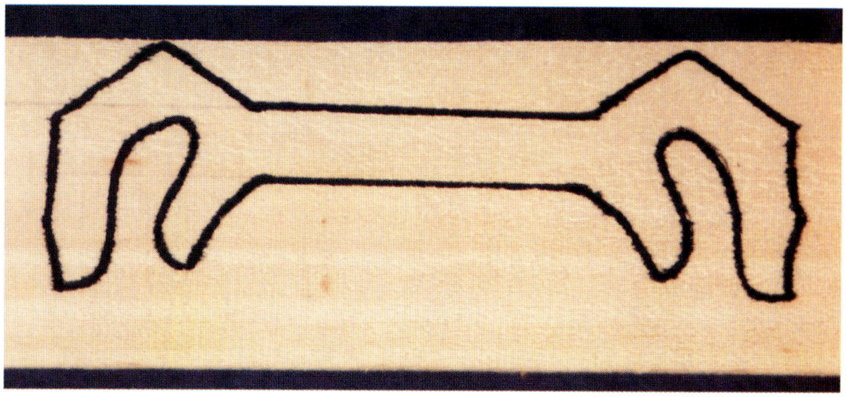

Transfer the top view of the hands to an appropriately-sized piece of wood. (For purposes of caricature, where exaggerations lend themselves to adding humor to the carving, the hands are a little larger than they would be in real life. This is the fun of carving caricatures versus real world anatomy...you have license to take liberties with features and proportions in order to achieve a more humorous effect). Notice that I have drawn in a strip of wood connecting the two hands. This will help form the wrist pins in a later step. Also, even though I will only carve one hand in the photos, they are both done the same way. Just make sure you get the thumbs oriented properly for each hand! Look at your own hands as a reference.

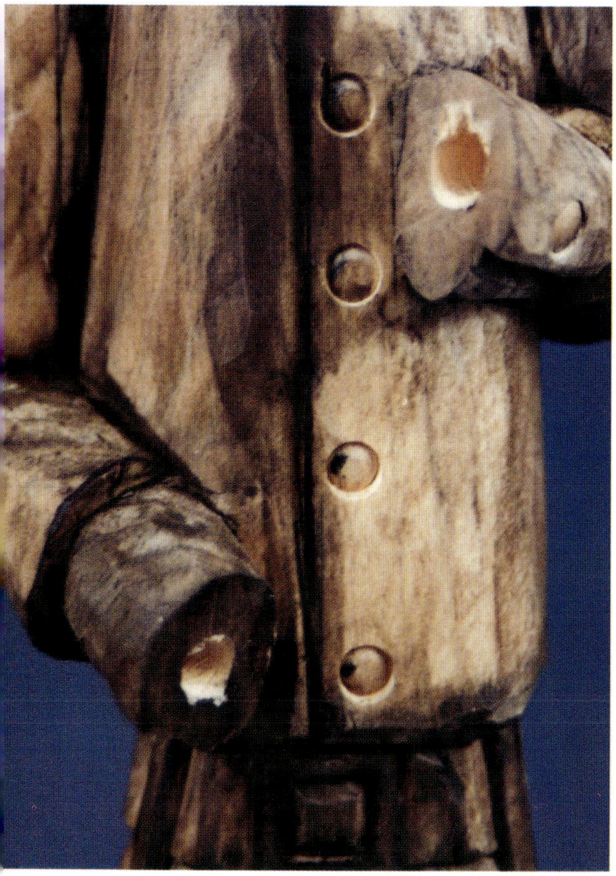

At this point, we have one step left to complete the body! We need to make some holes in the ends of the arms to receive the hands later. Using a 3/16" drill bit, drill holes about 3/8" deep centered in the ends of the arms.

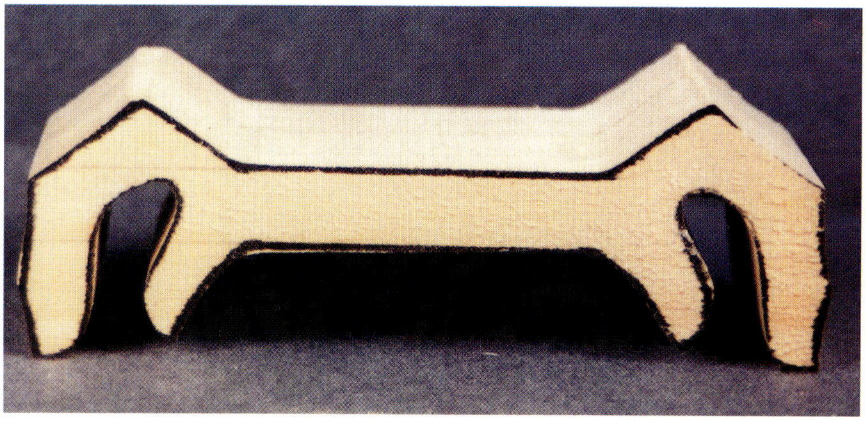

Saw out the top view.

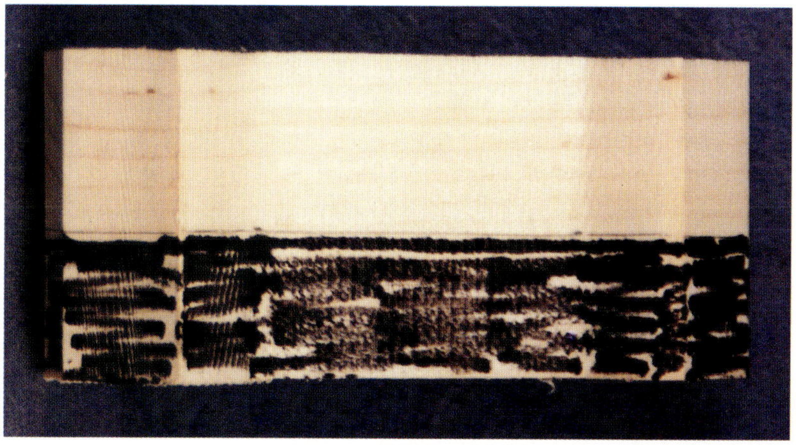

Rotate the hands 90° and measure in 1 1/8" from one of the edges. Draw a line to mark this. Saw away the excess wood. (It is the darkened wood in the photo).

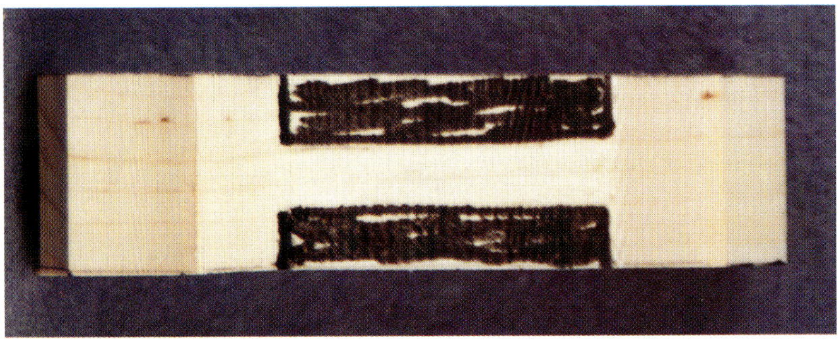

On the same side you made the last measurement, sketch the connecting strip between the two hands. The darkened area is to be sawn away.

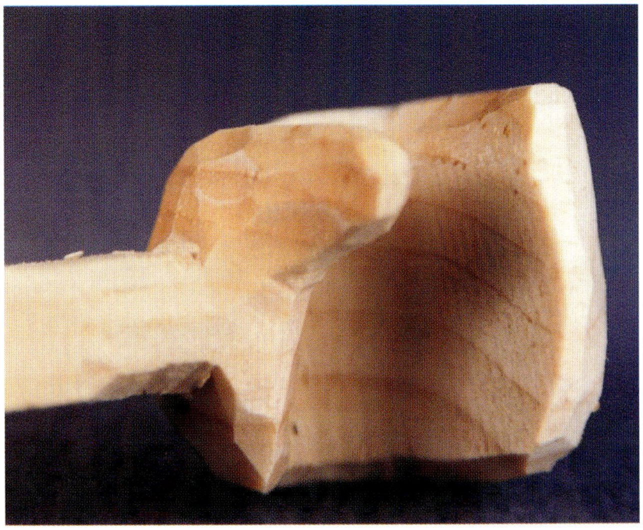

Remove the excess wood from the thumb area using your knife and 10mm "U" gouge, so the thumbs are well-defined. Round off any sharp edges remaining on the thumbs.

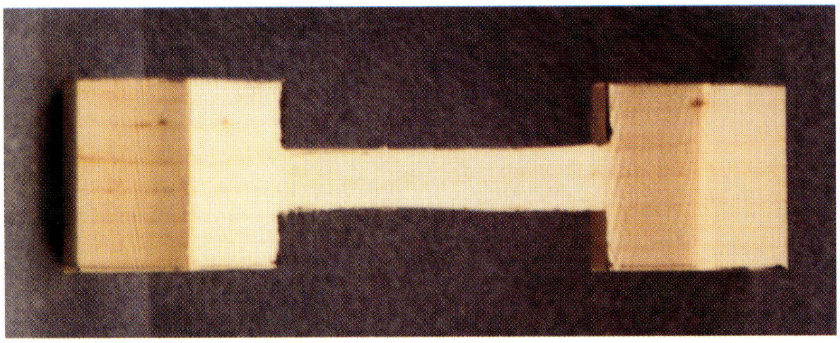

Here is how it looks with the wood removed. We now have a rough shape of the hands in both dimensions, side and top.

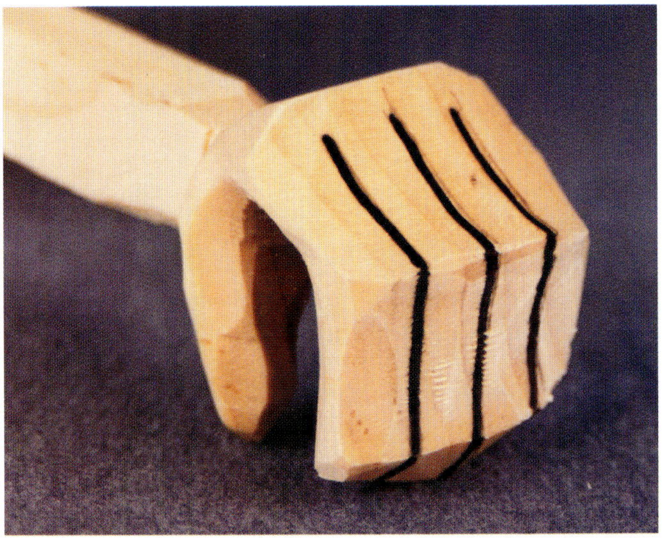

Draw a line in the middle of the finger section to divide it in half. Then, draw lines to divide each of these sections in half. You should now have four fingers defined, all approximately the same width.

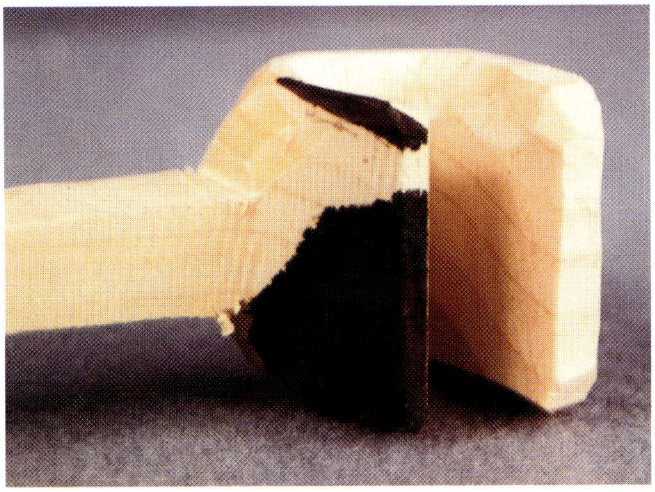

Use your knife to round off the sharp edges of the hands. Then sketch in the thumb. The darkened area is to be removed.

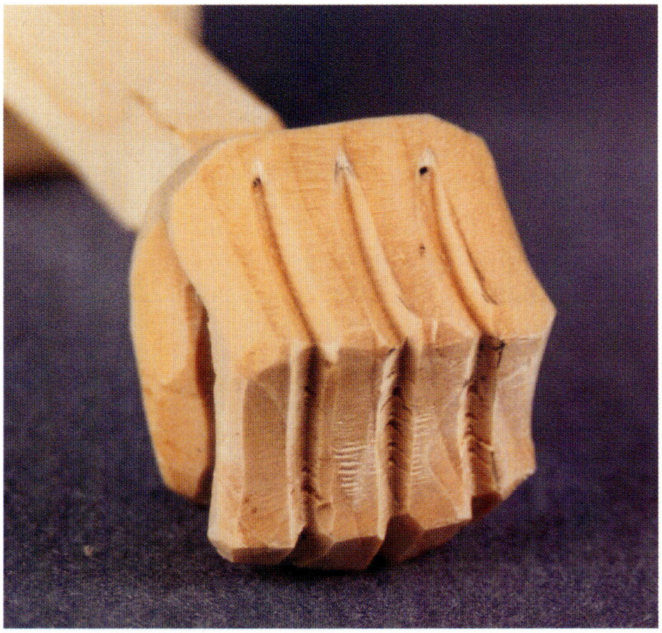

Use a 1/8" "V" gouge to go over these lines so the fingers will be separated. As an option, to add further detail without too much effort on your part, use a scroll saw or coping saw to carefully cut along these lines. Then, use your knife to remove any fuzzy wood caused by the saw cuts. More advanced carvers can add other details as desired, such as knuckles and wrinkles on the finger joints.

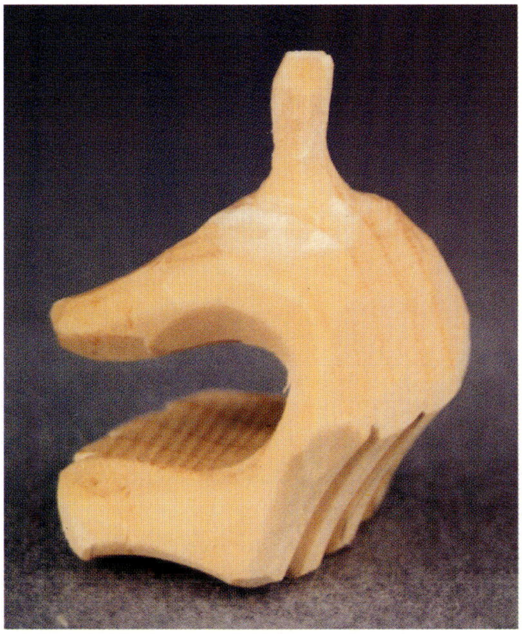

Next, saw or cut the hands apart, but leave a section of the connecting strip attached to each hand. Using your knife, trim the section of wood down to form a "wrist" that will fit snugly into the holes you drilled earlier into the ends of the arms. When done properly, the hand will appear to be coming out of the sleeve. This method allows you more freedom to turn the hands in different directions, and allows you to use the grain of the wood to your benefit. After we paint the hands, we'll attach them.

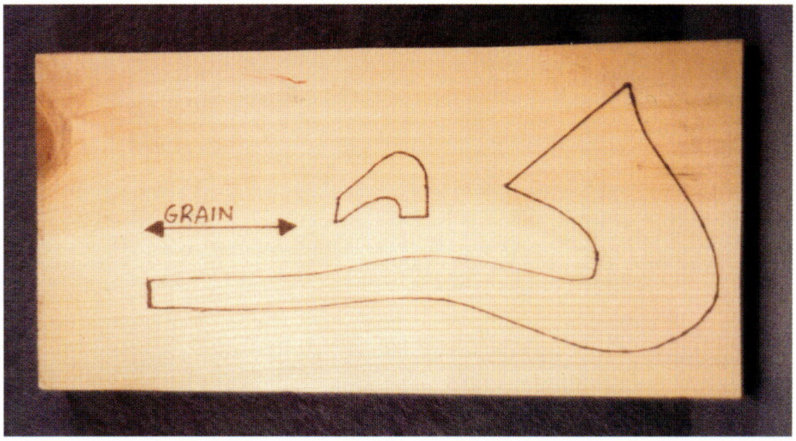

Transfer the saxophone pattern (body and mouthpiece) to a 1 1/2" thick piece of wood.

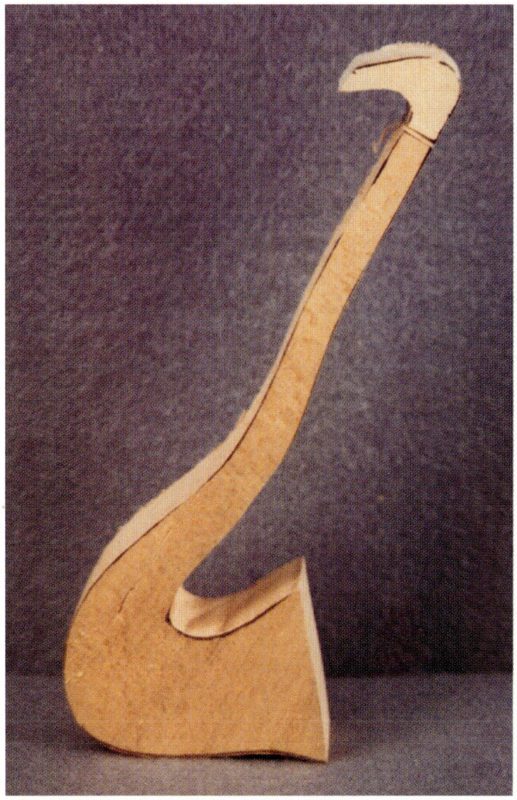

Saw out both pieces and glue them together, centering the mouthpiece assembly on the thicker body section as shown. Let the glue dry for at least 12 hours before proceeding.

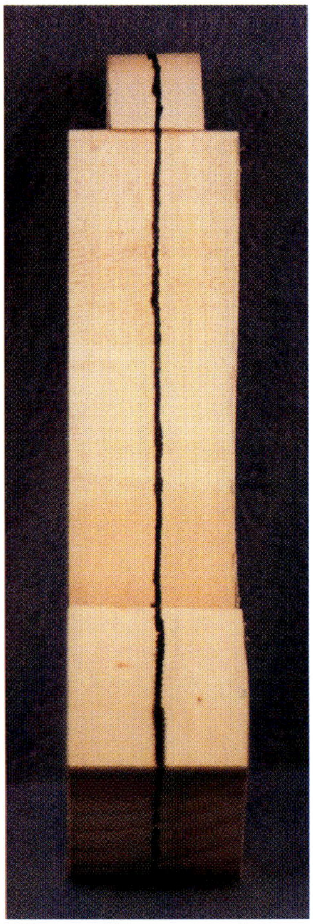

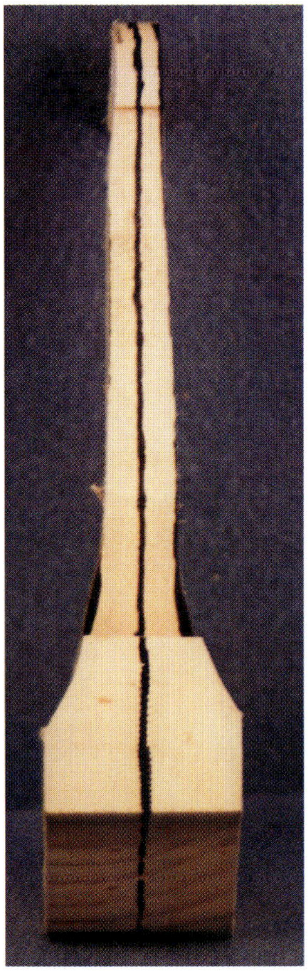

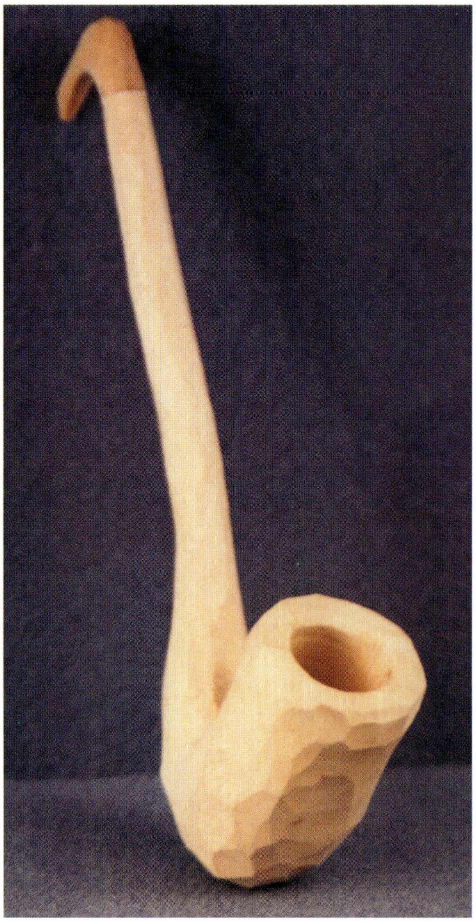

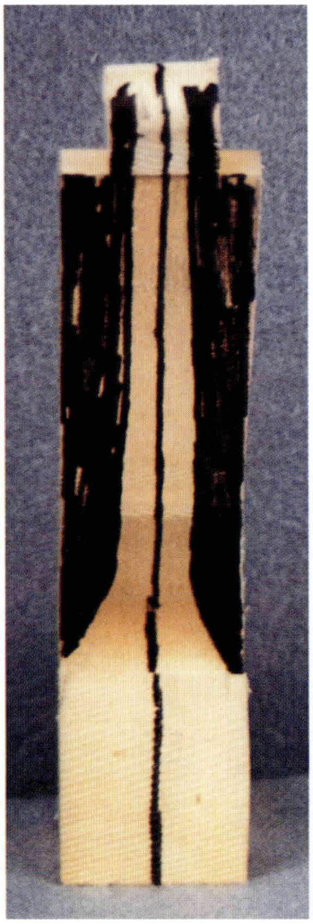

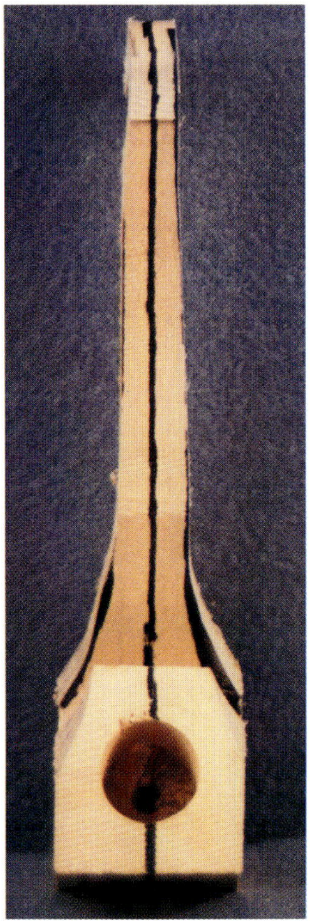

Top left: Sketch a reference line down the approximate center of the assembly.

Bottom left: Now, measure out about 1/8" from each side of the center line at the top of the saxophone. Then, sketch in lines from there to the outside edges of the "bell" at the bottom of the sax. This will define the rough shape of the sax, and will take away some of the hard work in the final shaping of it. The darkened wood will be carefully sawn away. Notice how the lines "flare" out as they reach the bell end of the sax.

Top center: Saw away the excess wood, following the lines you drew, to arrive at this shape.

Bottom center: If you wish to add a bit of detail to the bell end of the sax, use a 3/4" drill bit (wood-boring bit) to remove some wood and create a hole down into the bell. Hurricane needs a way to get those mellow tones out of his sax!

Top right: As you did on the arms, legs and other parts of the body, use your knife to round off the sax. First knock off all four sharp edges, then keep removing sharp edges until you have reached a state of roundness you are happy with. Sounds like some kind of Zen philosophy, doesn't it? Now, when you *think* you are done, test-fit the sax in the hands to make sure it fits between the fingers and thumb of each hand. Trim wood as needed until you get a good fit. This keeps from having to remove wood later, after the painting is all done!

That's it!! All the carving work is finished. All we have to do now is paint, antique, varnish and assemble this rascal. While I'm thinking of it, before I start painting, I'm going to make a base for him to stand on. This can be anything of your choosing. I am going to use a section of wood 3" x 3" x 1 1/2" thick, and stain it a light Walnut. You can use a stain or paint color of your choice.

Painting the Project

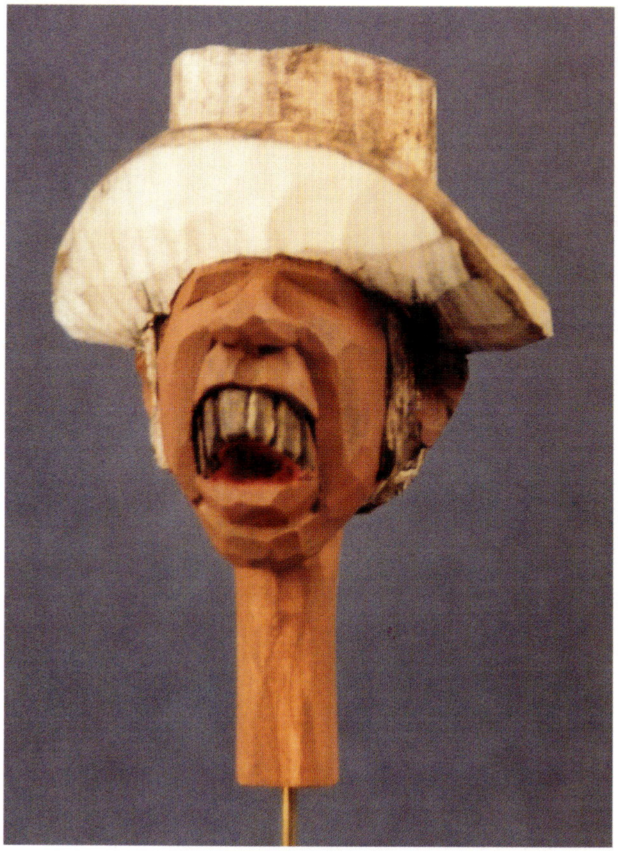

The face, neck, ears and hands are painted Light Cinnamon. While the face is still damp, lightly blend in a small amount of DeLane's Cheek Color on the cheeks, inside the mouth, and on the lower lip.

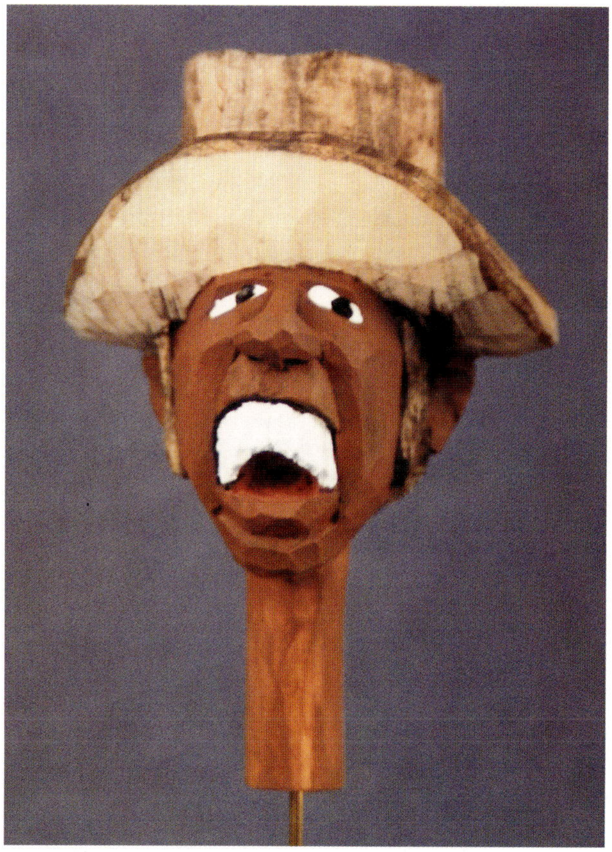

The eye grooves and teeth are Titanium White. When the eyes are dry, put a small dot of Lamp Black near the left corner of both eyes.

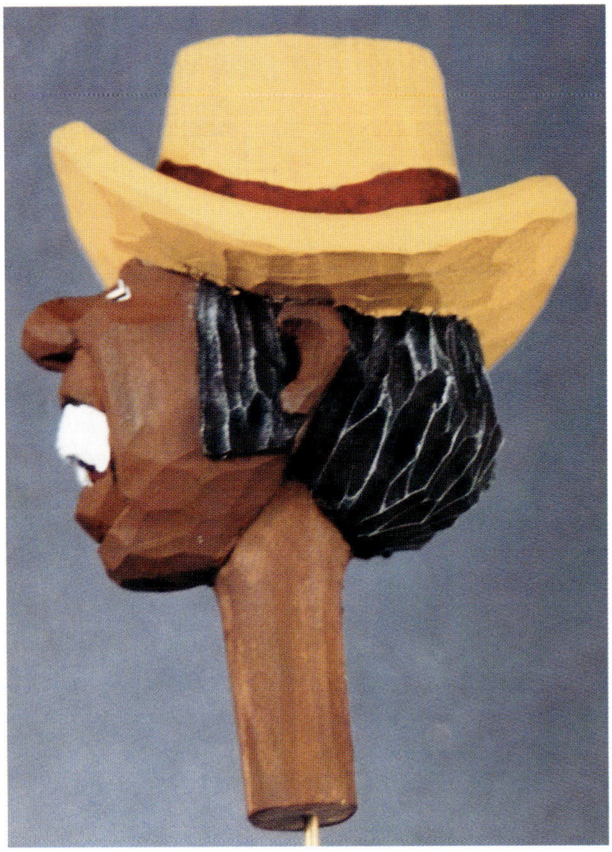

The hair is Lamp Black. When it is dry, lightly dry-brush over it with Titanium White to just catch the high spots, and give a little "age' to ol' Hurricane.

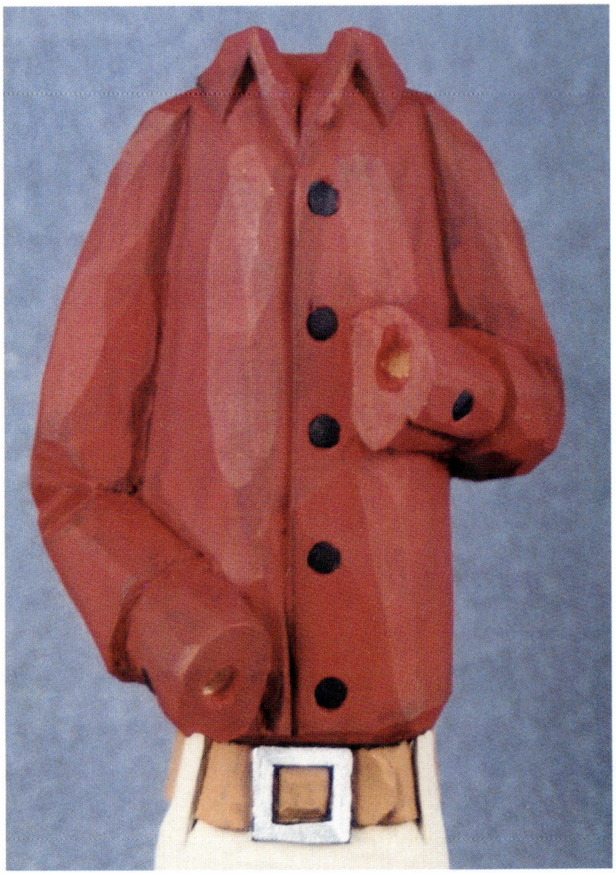

The shirt is Calico Red, Lamp Black buttons.

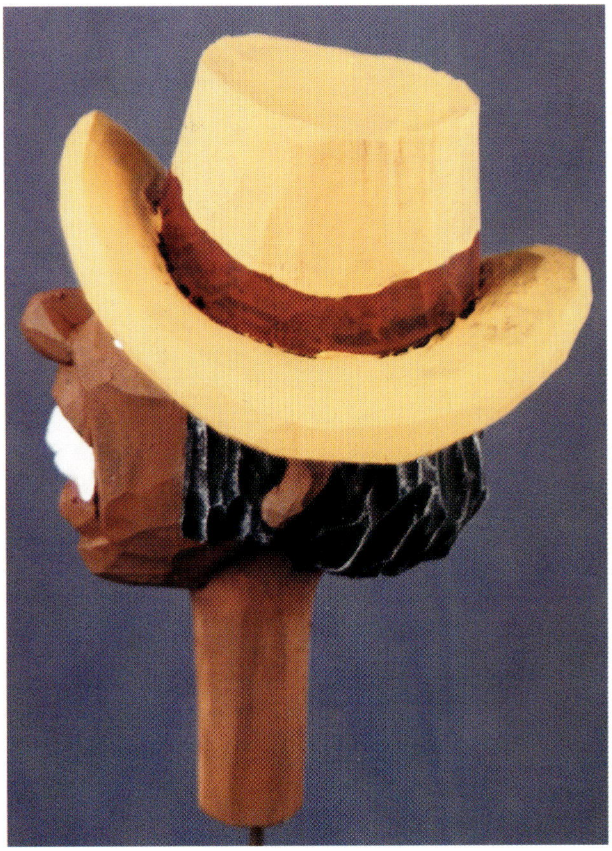

The hat is Marigold, with a Calico Red hat band.

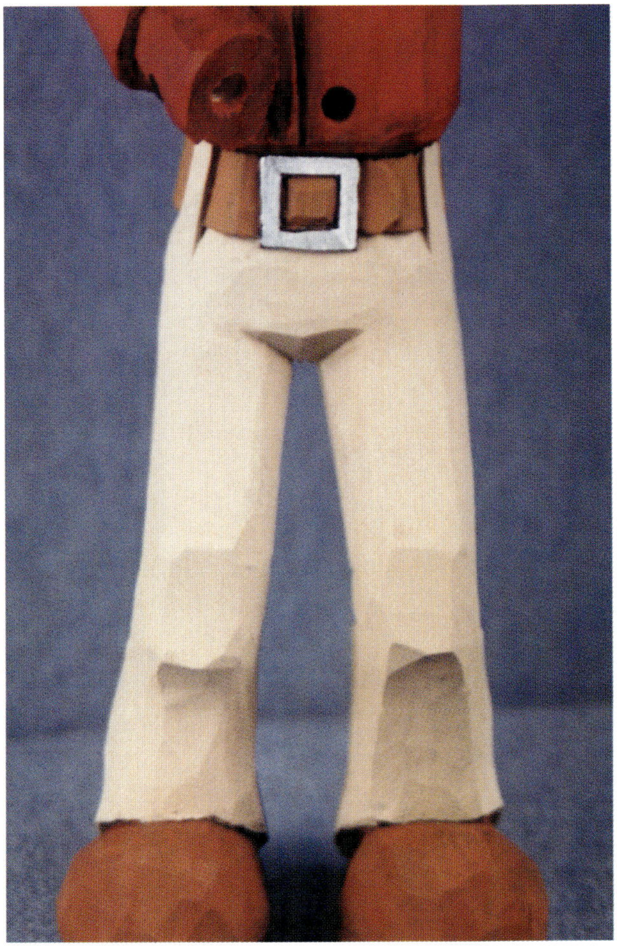

The pants are Khaki Tan.

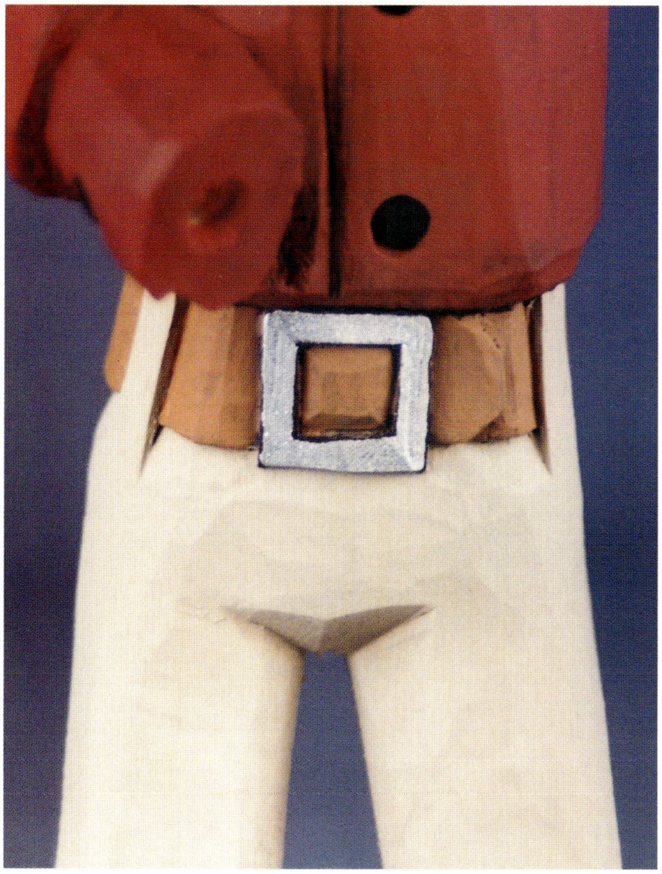

The belt is Raw Sienna with a Brilliant Silver buckle.

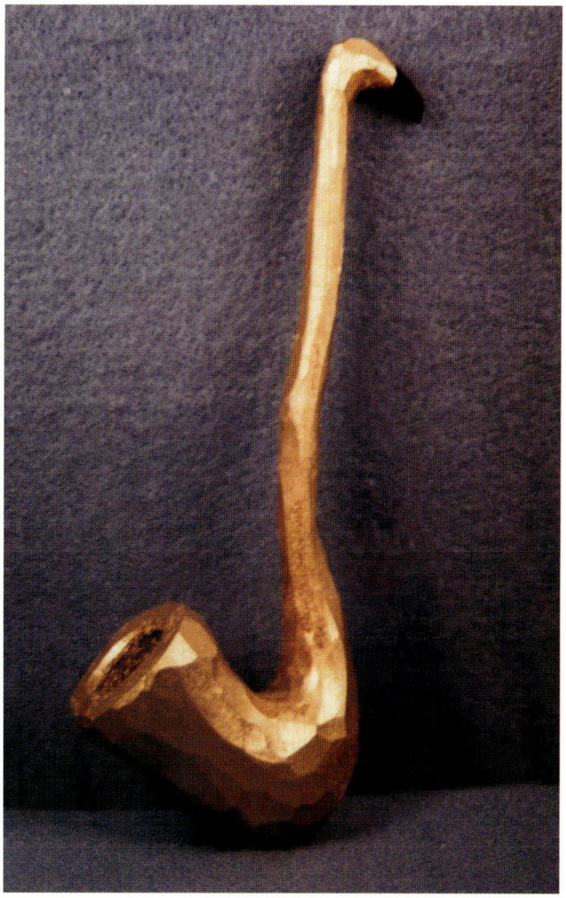

And the saxophone is Royal Gold with a Lamp Black mouthpiece.

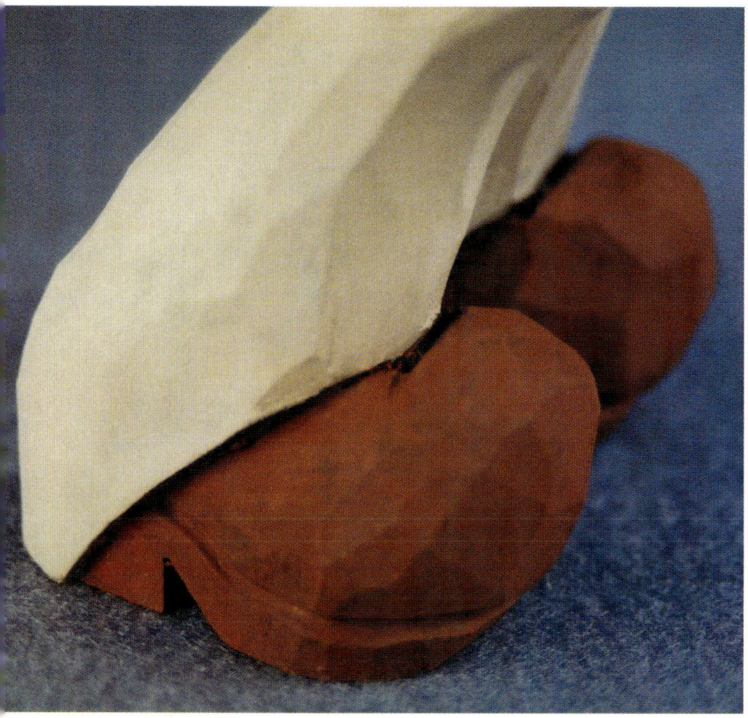

The shoes are Burnt Sienna.

After all the paint is dry, tone down the colors by 'antiquing' the pieces. I used Walnut gel stain. Brush it on the wood, then use a damp cloth to remove the excess. This will soften the colors. Finally, use Satin Varnish to seal all the pieces.

To assemble the project, read this carefully before proceeding: Insert the right hand into the arm, but do not glue it yet. Next, insert the sax into the right hand. Place the left hand around the sax and insert it into the left arm. When everything is lined up, carefully slide out one hand at a time. Put a drop of glue on the wrist pin, and re-insert the hand back into the arm. Position the sax as you like it, then put a small drop of glue inside each hand to secure it. Let the assembly dry several hours before proceeding.

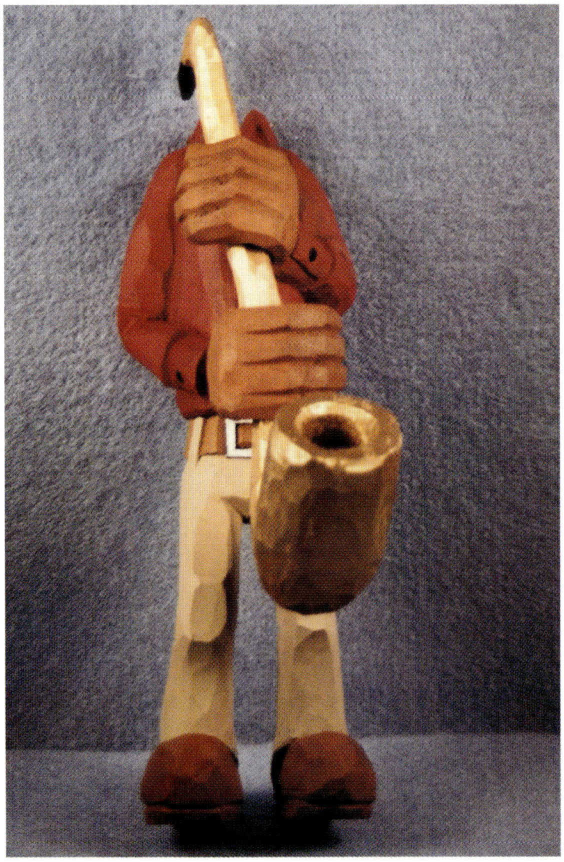

At this point, your project should resemble this.

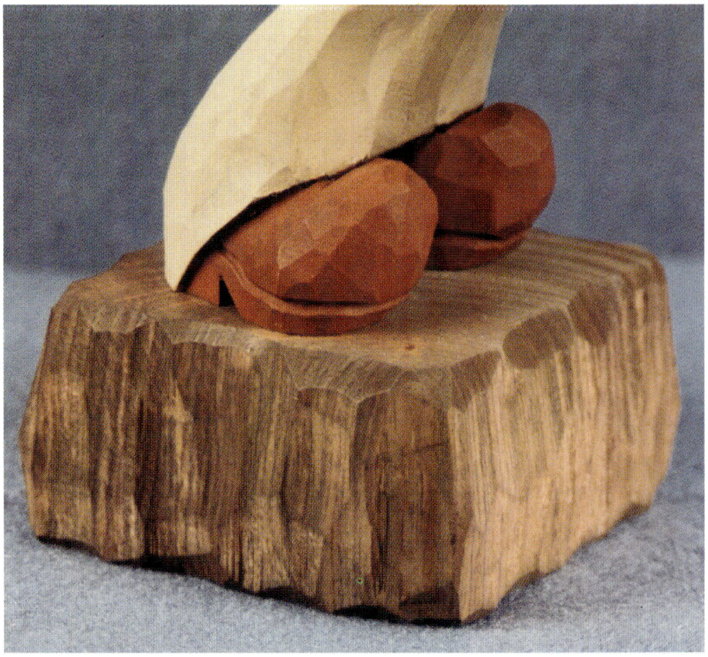

Glue the carving to its base, and this job is done.

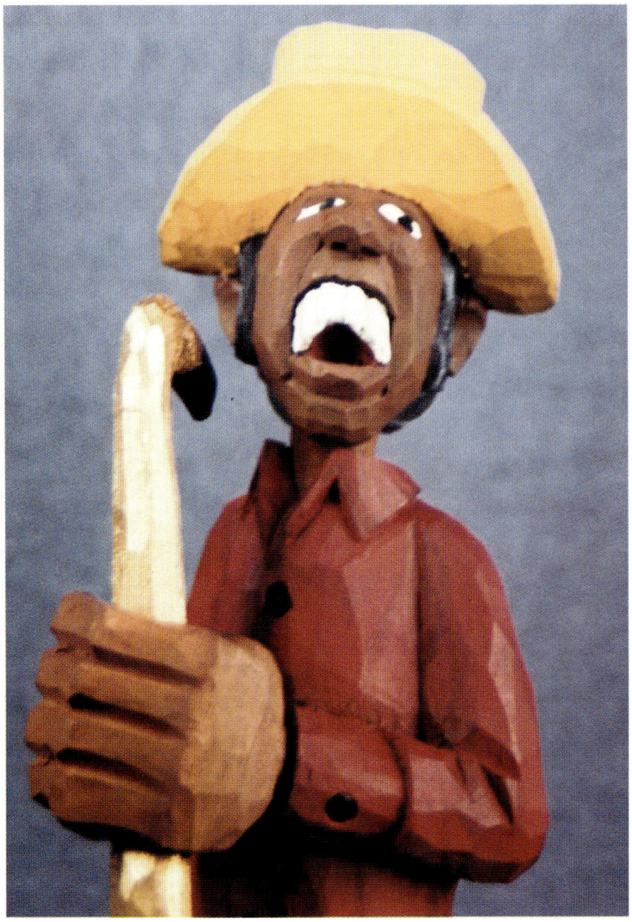

Put a drop or two of glue in the neck hole, and insert the head. Your project will have more "life" to it if you will turn the head to one side slightly.

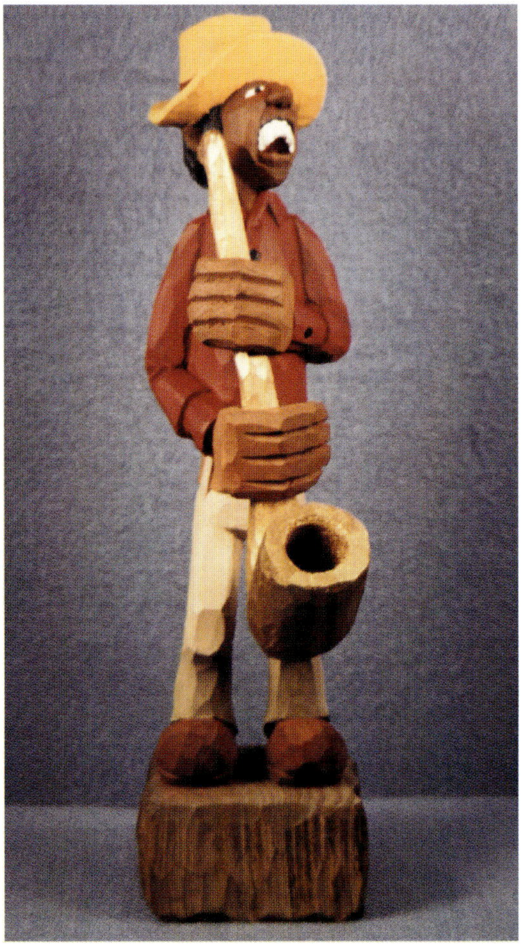

Front view of the completed project.

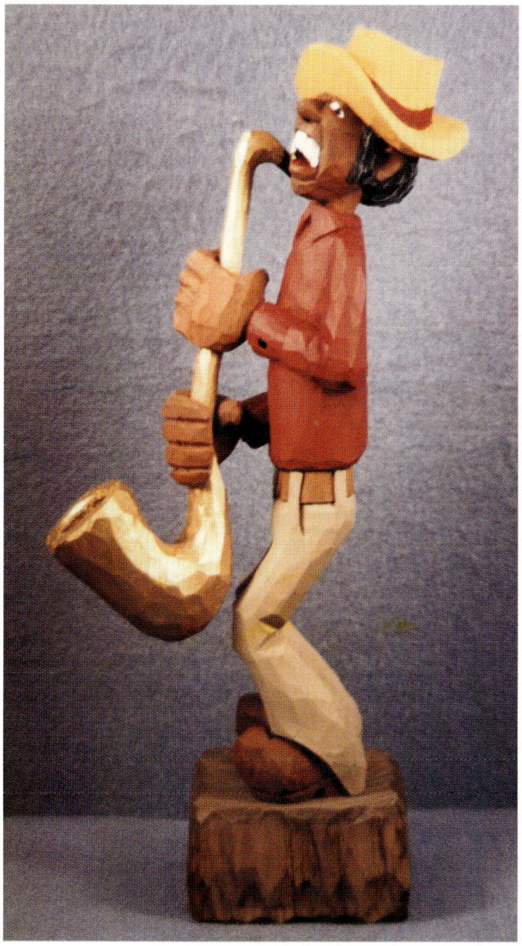

Left view of the completed project.

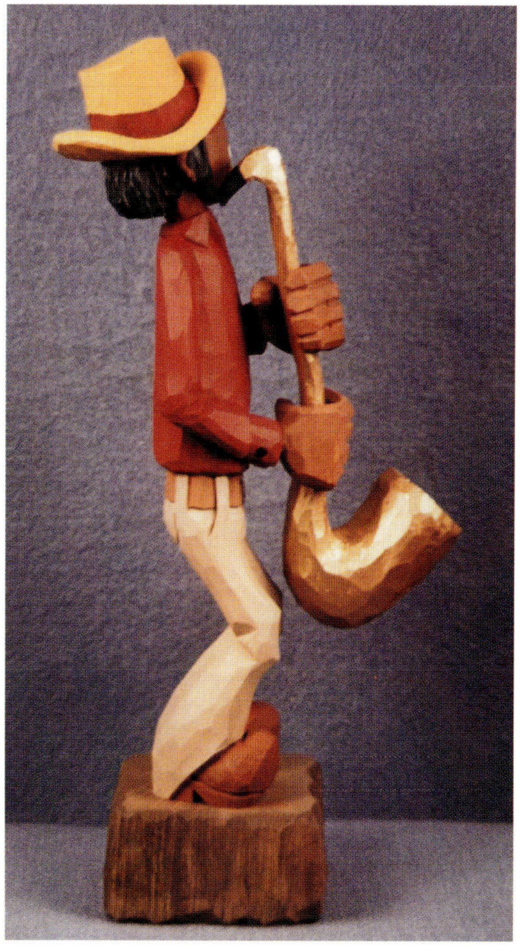

Right view of the completed project.

Rear view of the completed project.

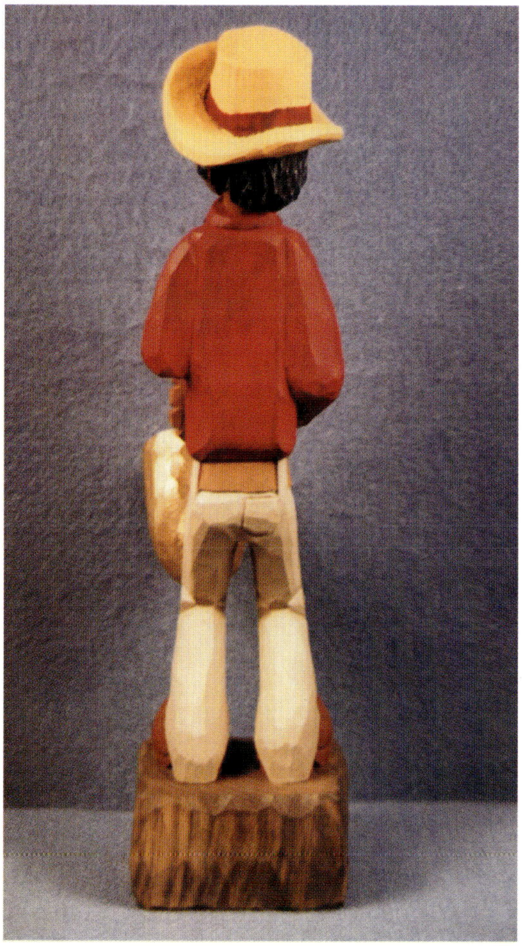

For posterity, you should sign, number and date your carving. This makes it more valuable to the collectors who will be seeking out your work some day, if not already. I hope that in some way I have been able to help each of you with some aspect of carving and painting. When we share tips and information, we all become better. If you have any comments or questions about something in this book, or if you have an idea you'd like to see me put in a future book, please feel free to write, e-mail, or call me at the following address and telephone number. I welcome any comments or suggestions you have.

Al Streetman
402 North Broad Street
Guthrie, Oklahoma 73044
(405) 282-8234
astreetman@mmcable.com

Gallery and Study Models

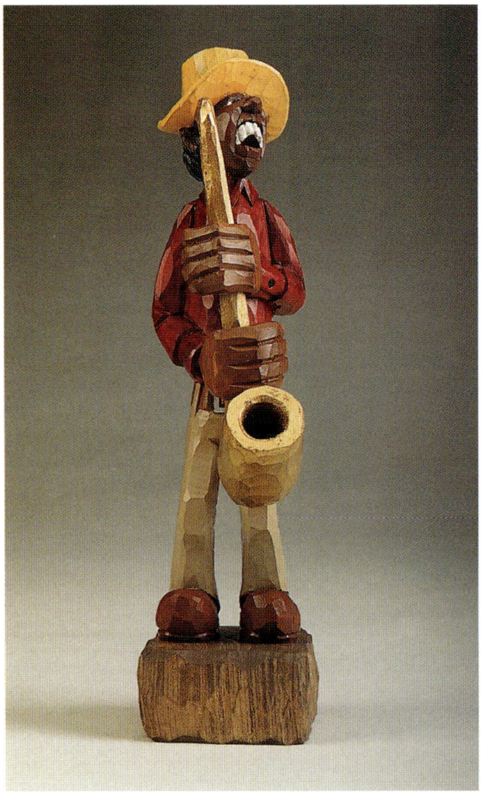

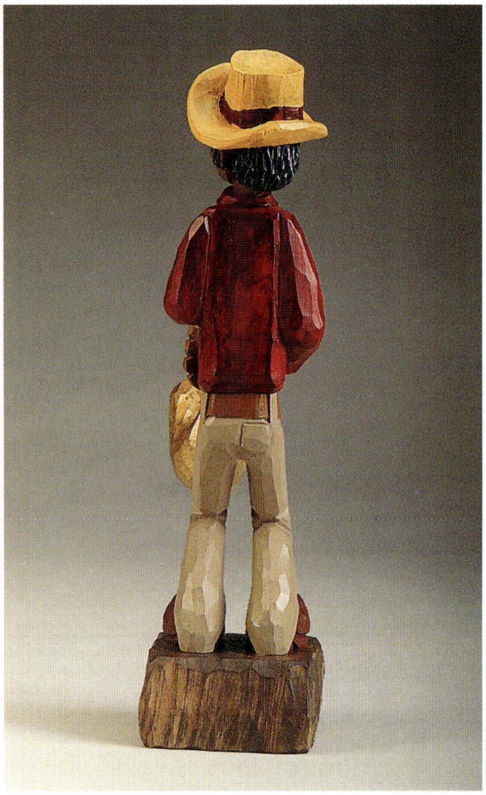

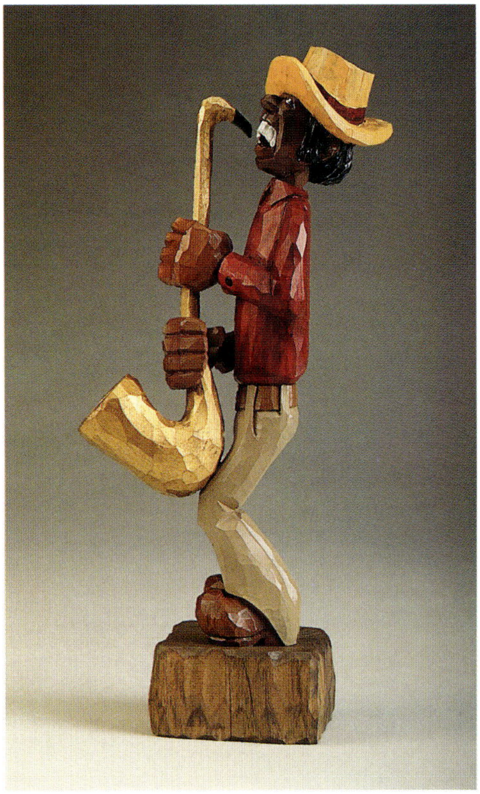

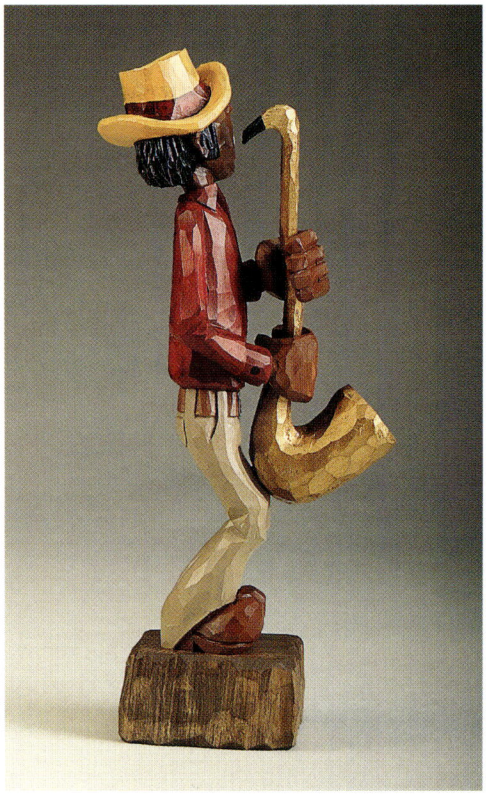

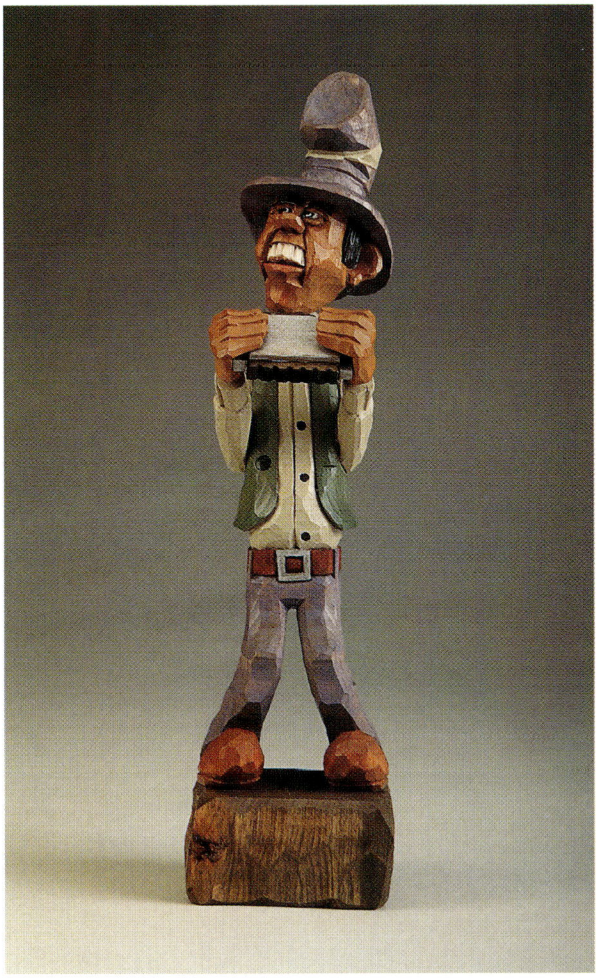
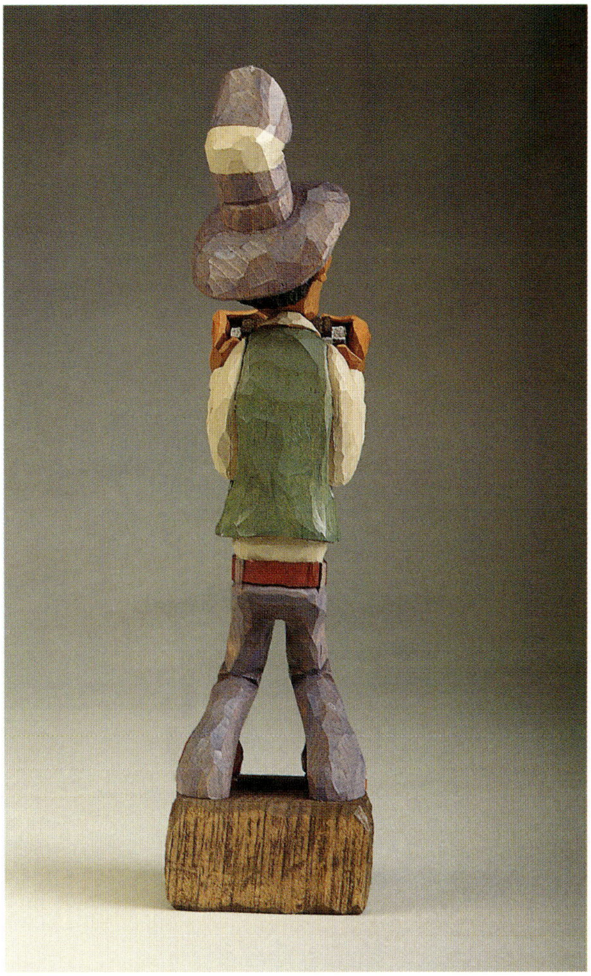
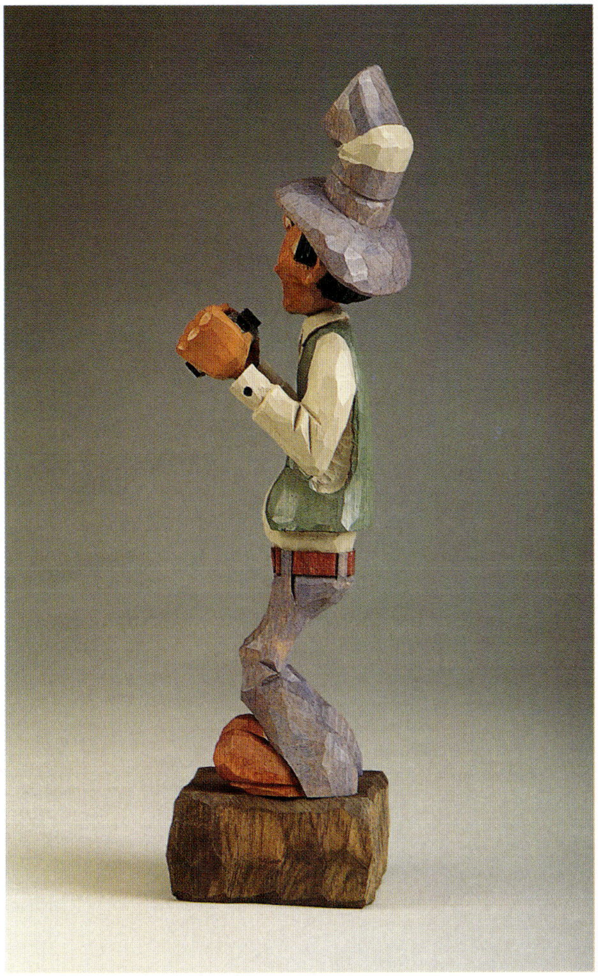
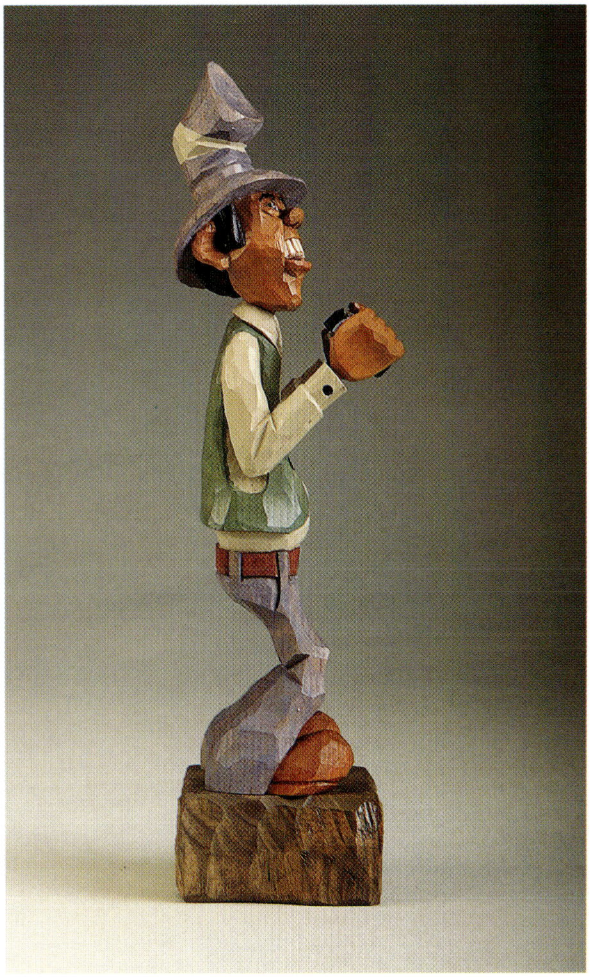

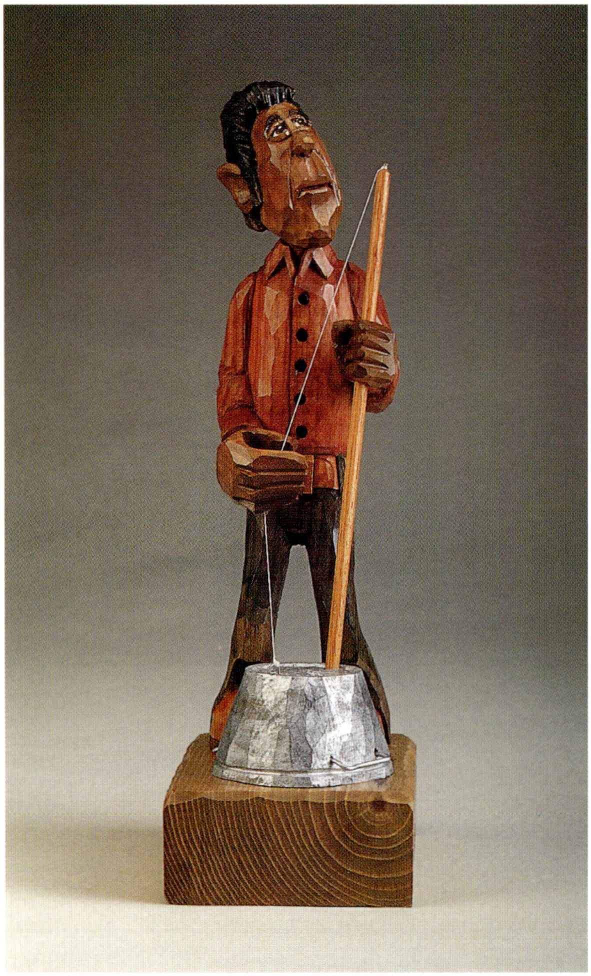
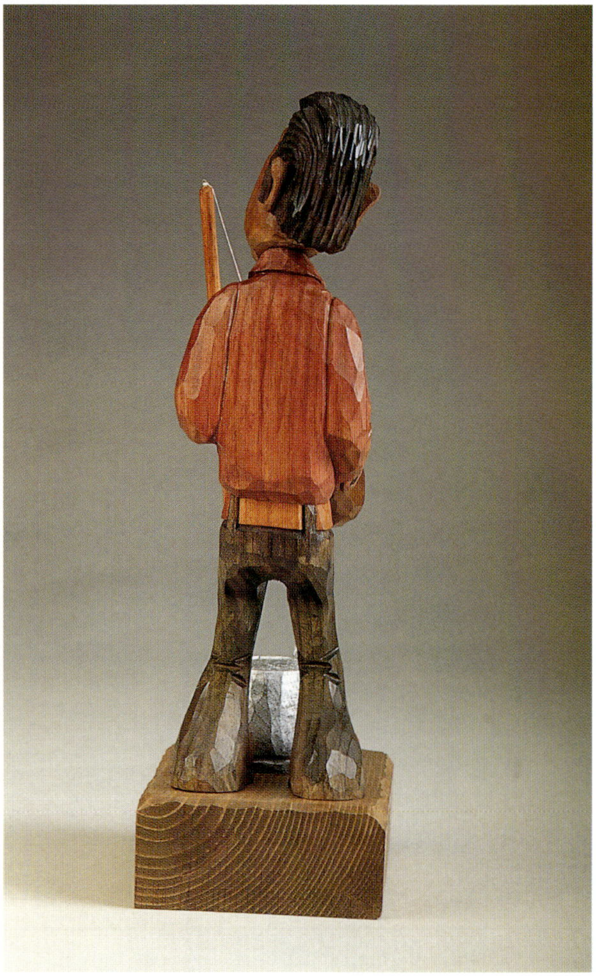
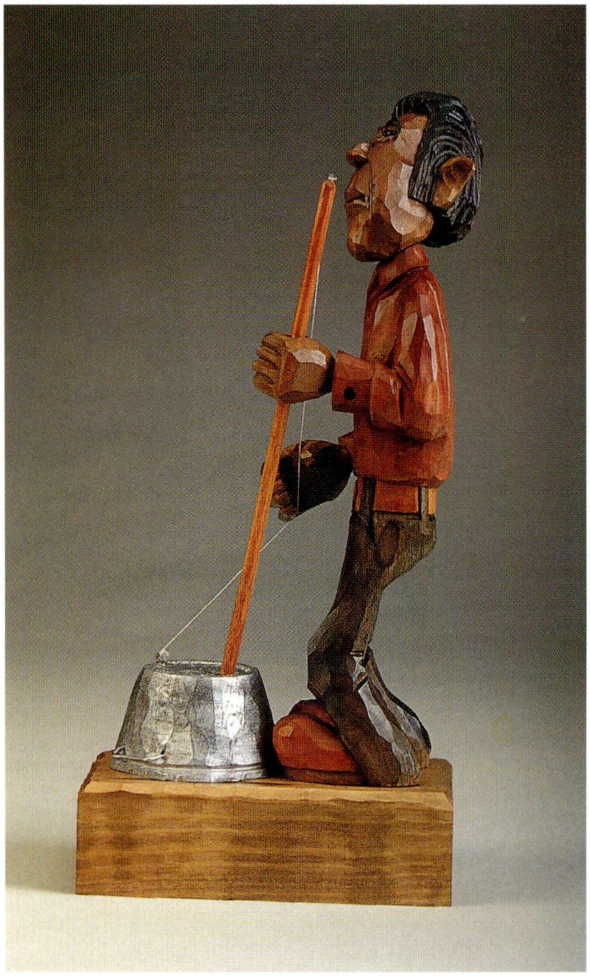
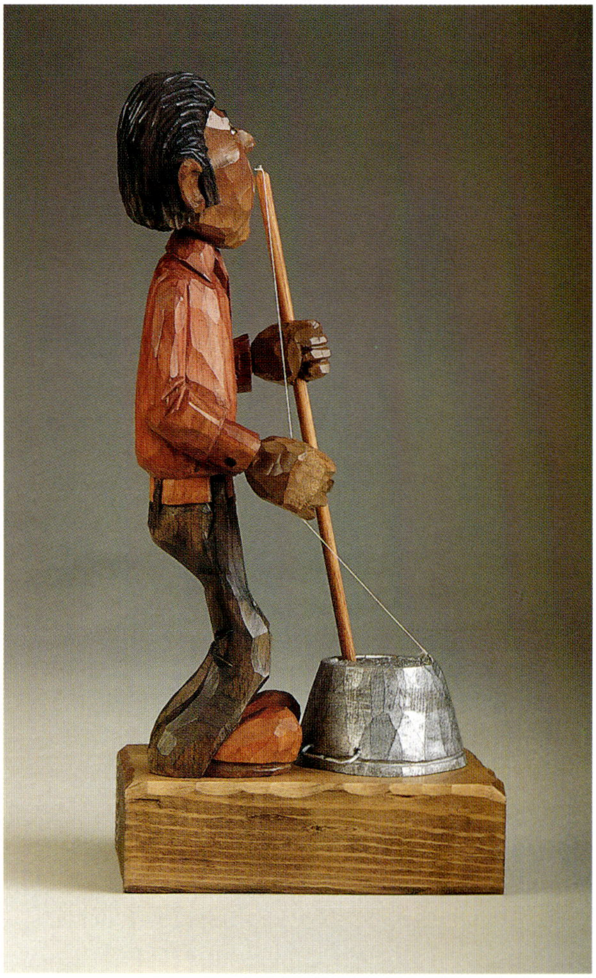

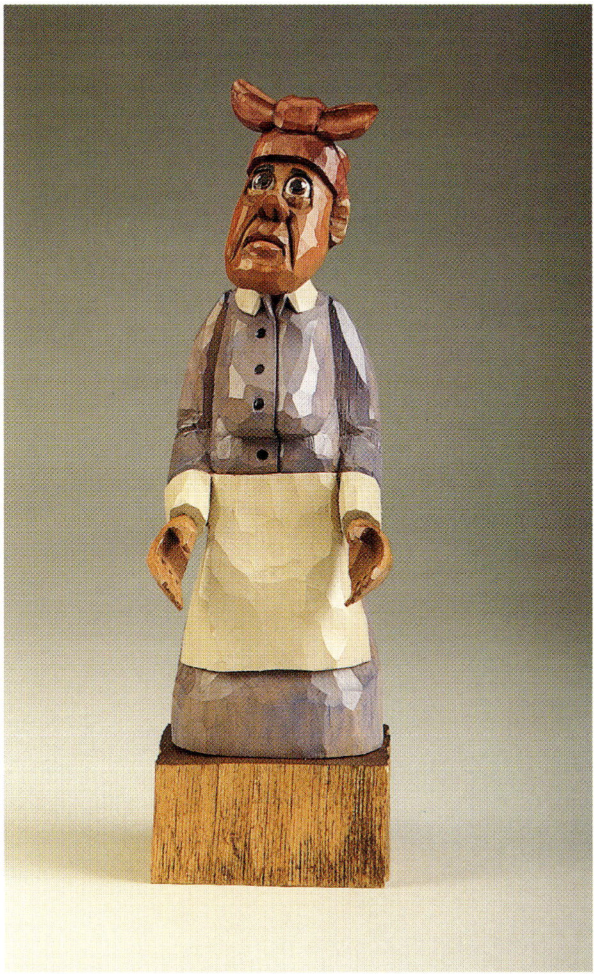
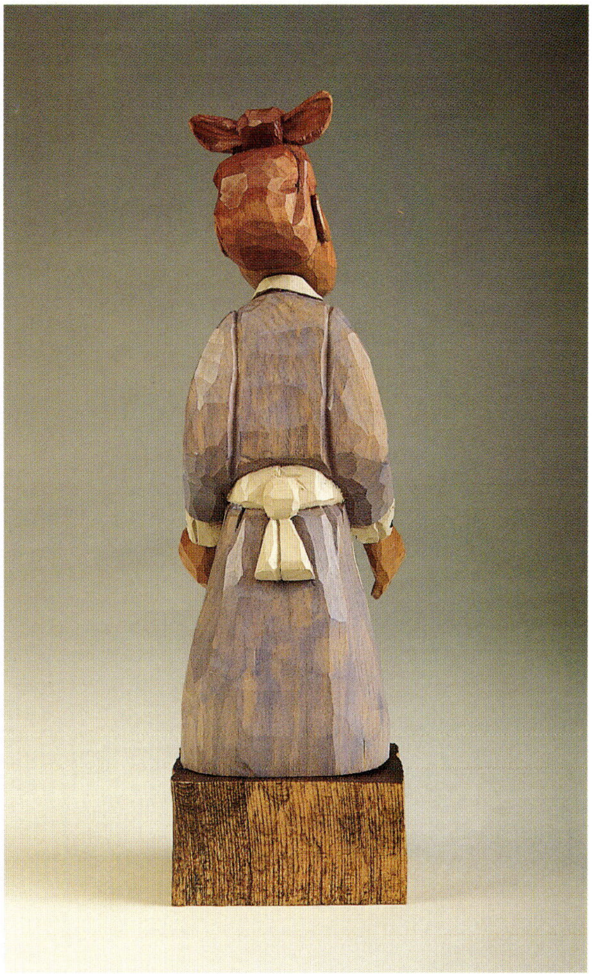
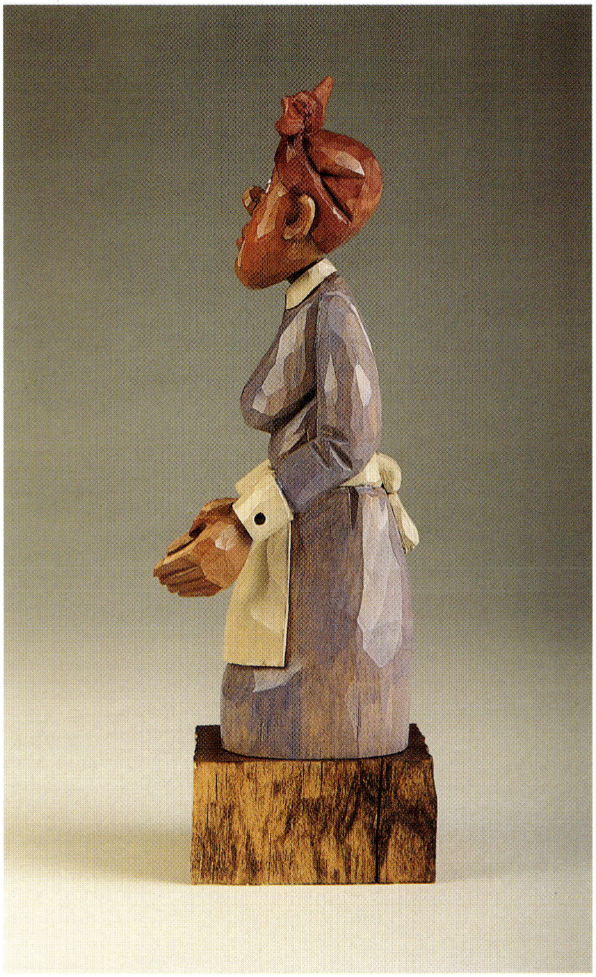
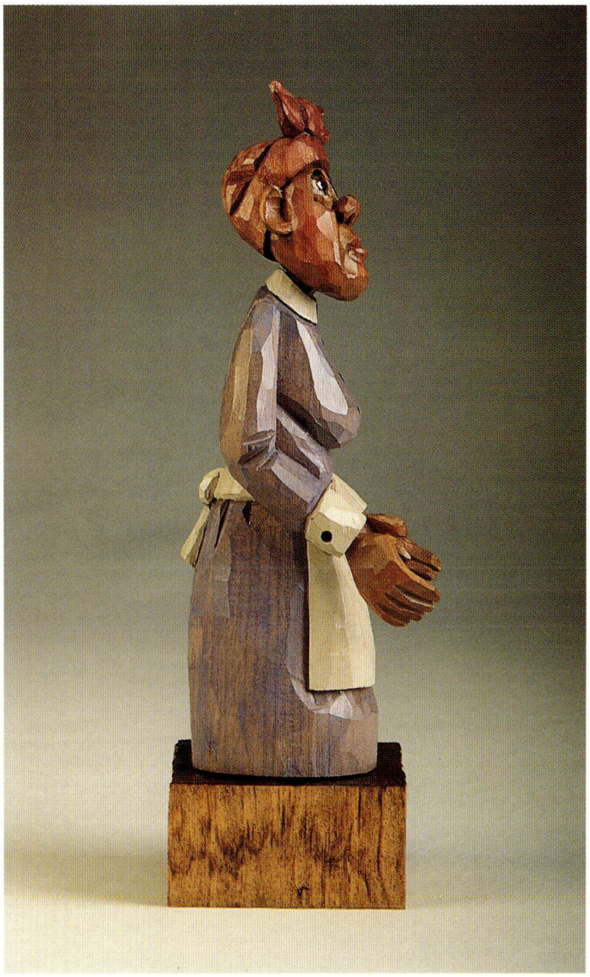

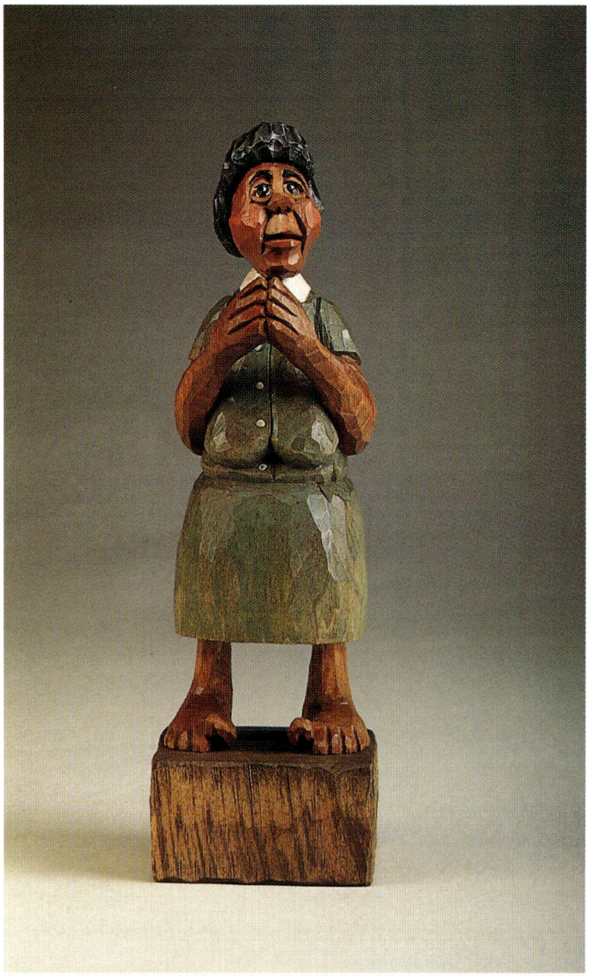
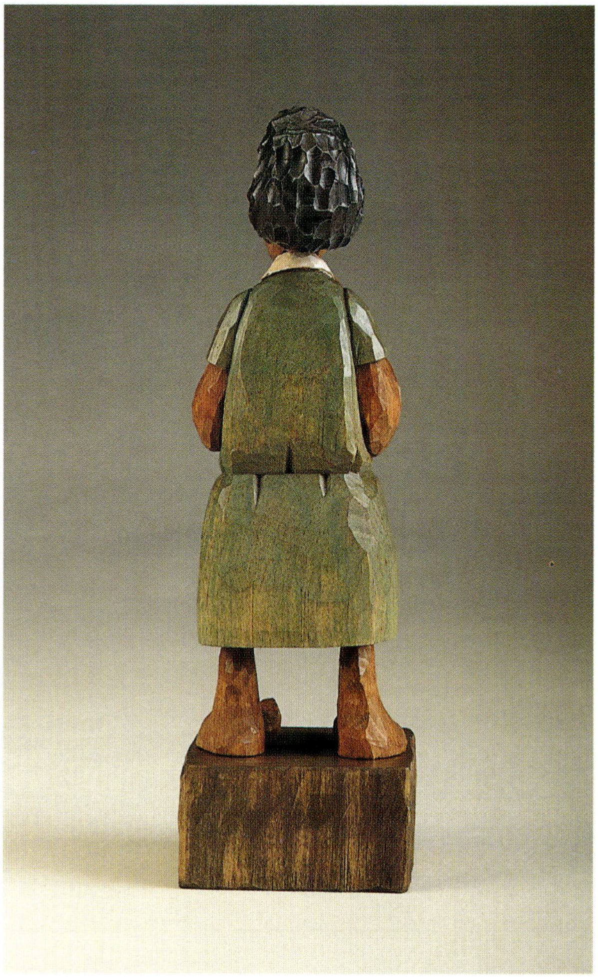
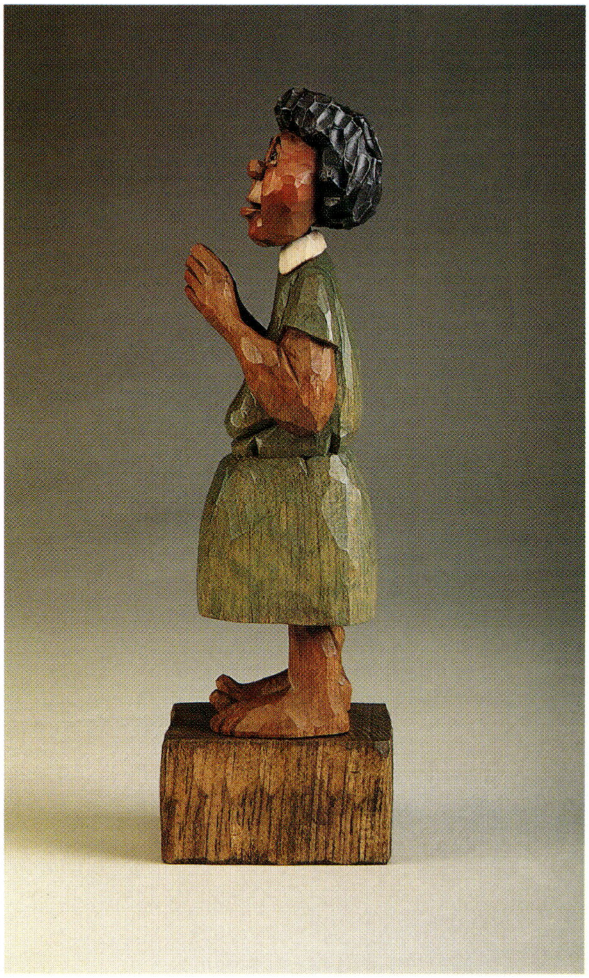
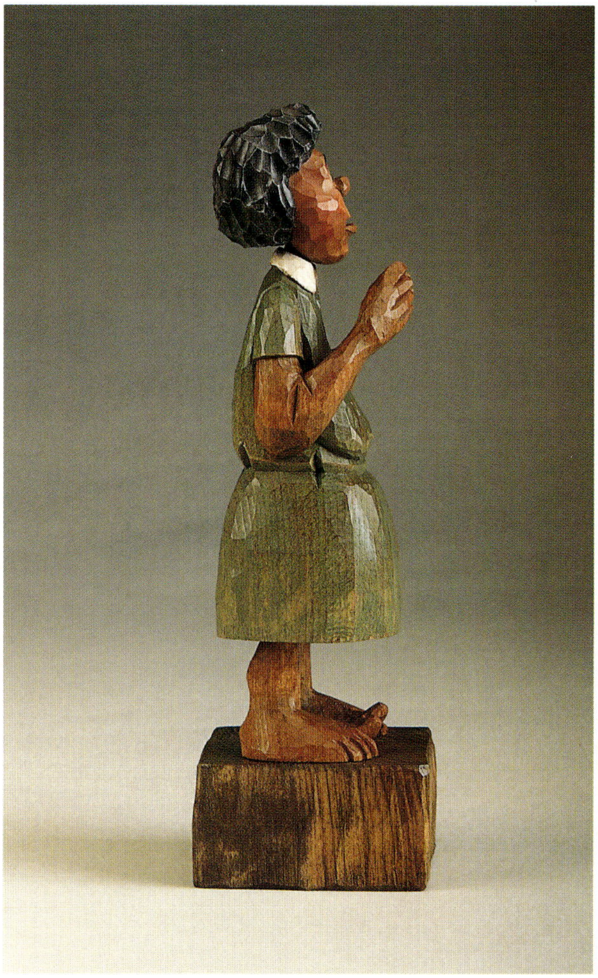

Patterns

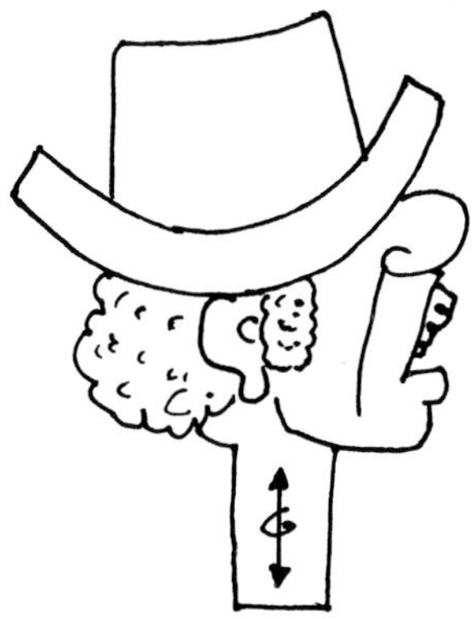

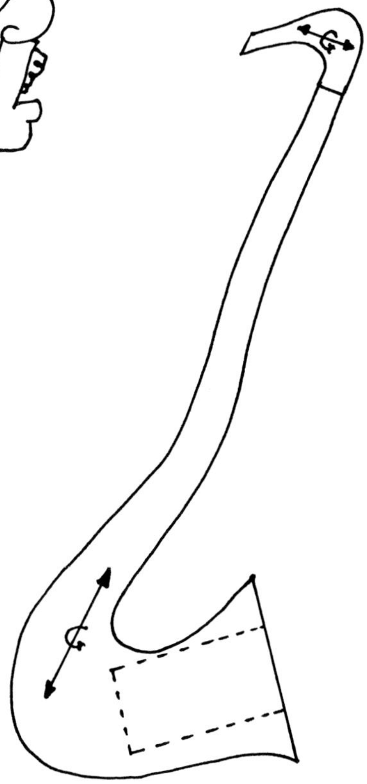

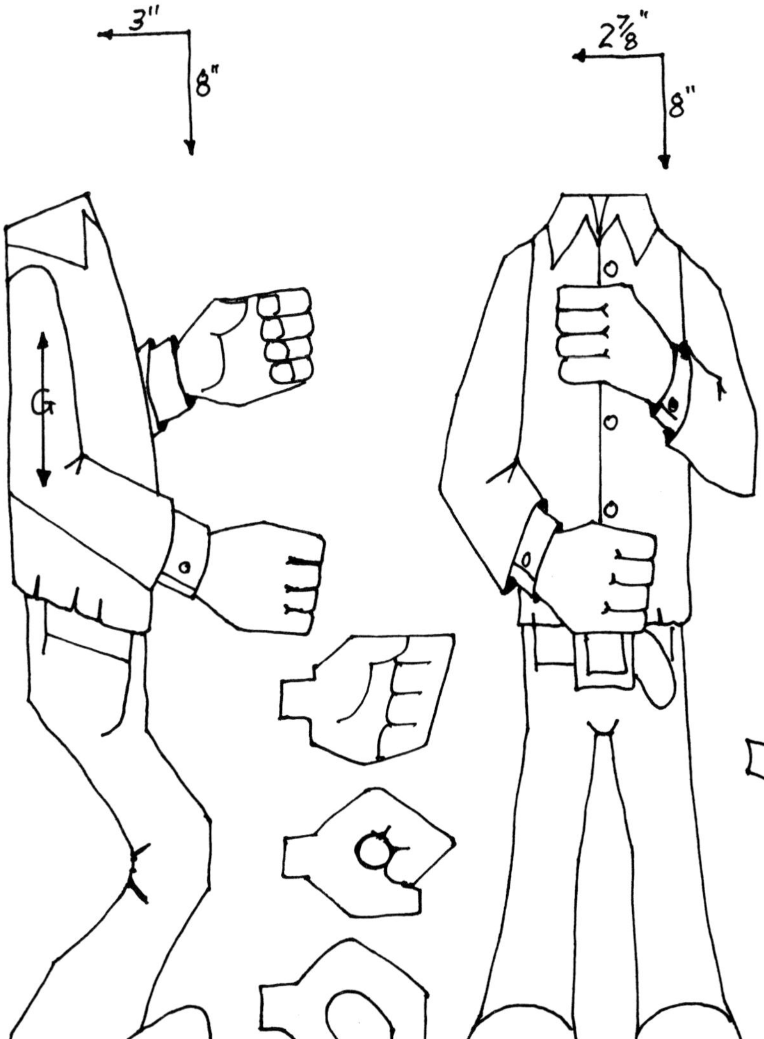

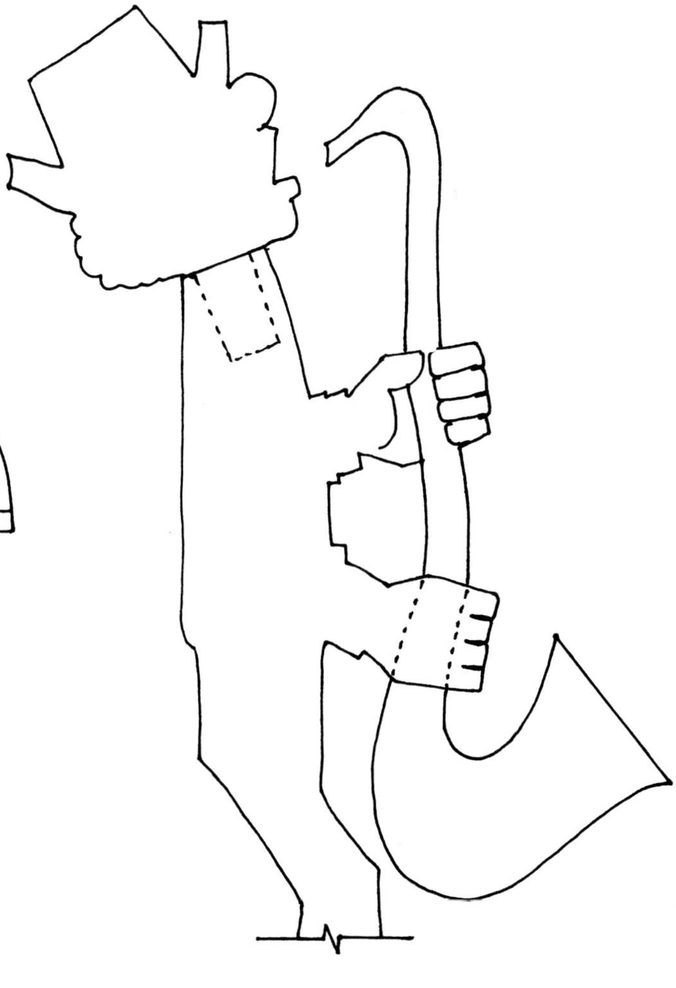

Hurricane Brown

Note: Patterns have been reduced.
Enlarge to 166% for actual size.

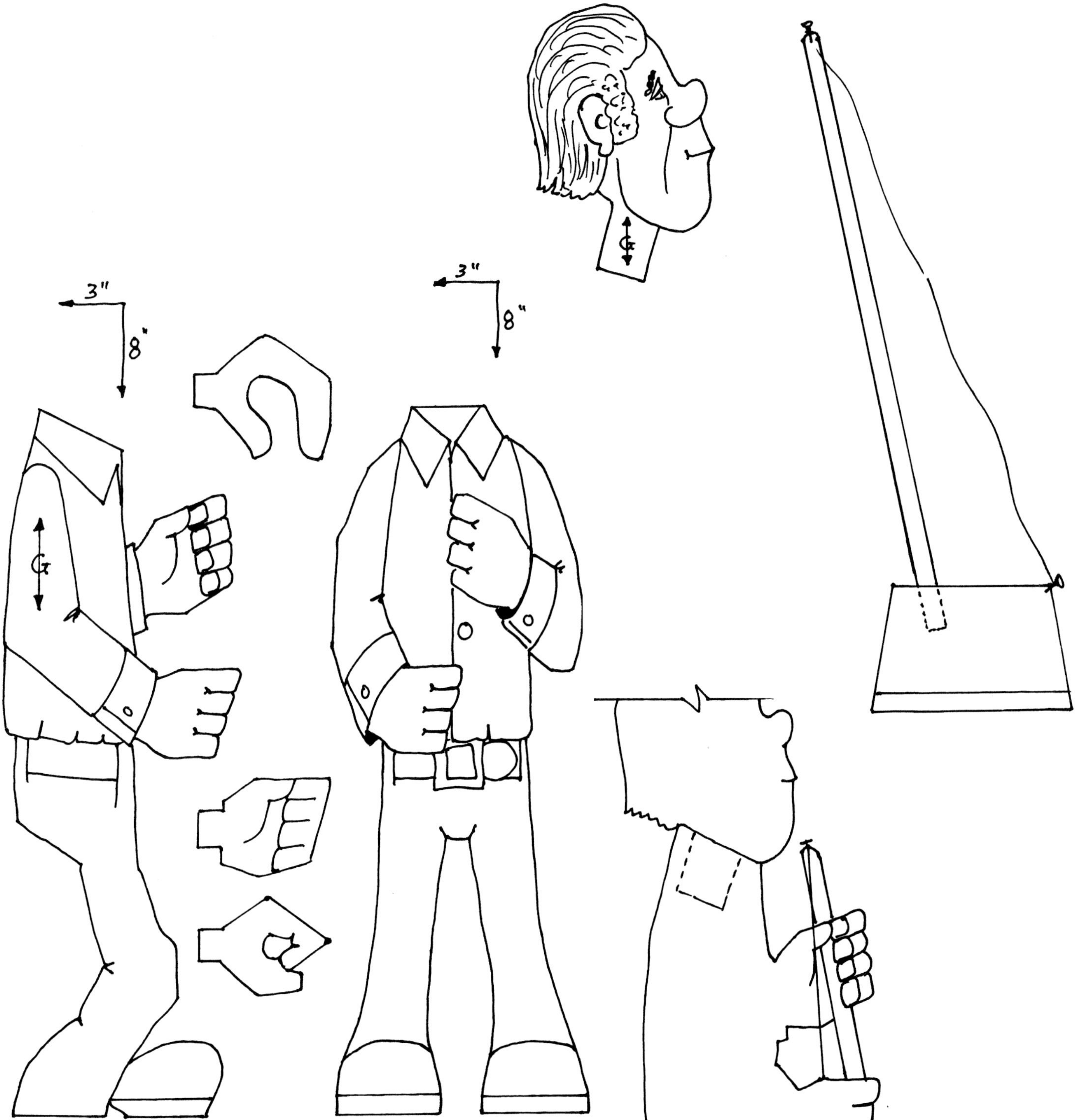

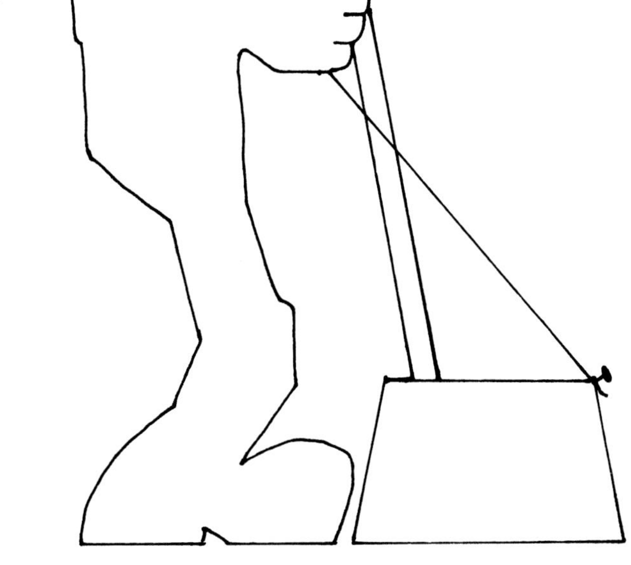

"Junior" Tillman

Note: Patterns have been reduced.
Enlarge to 166% for actual size.

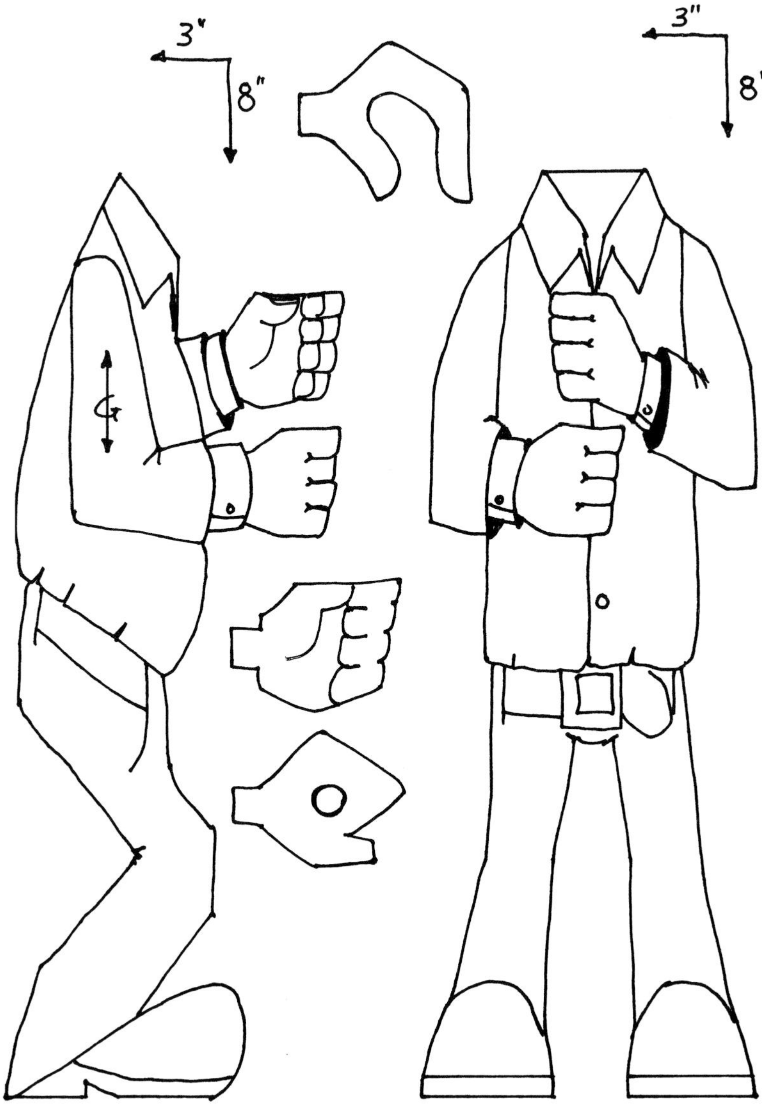

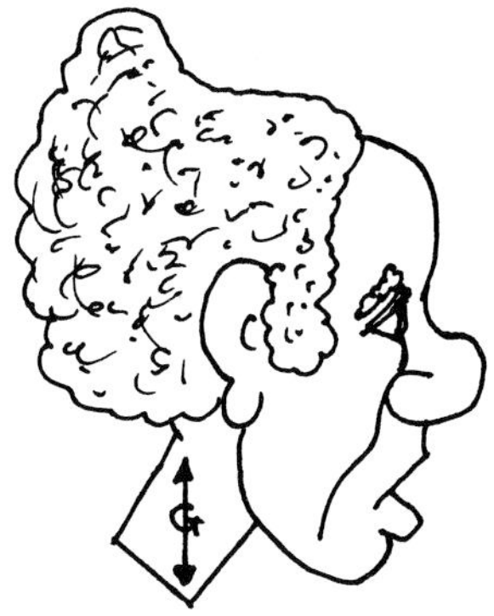

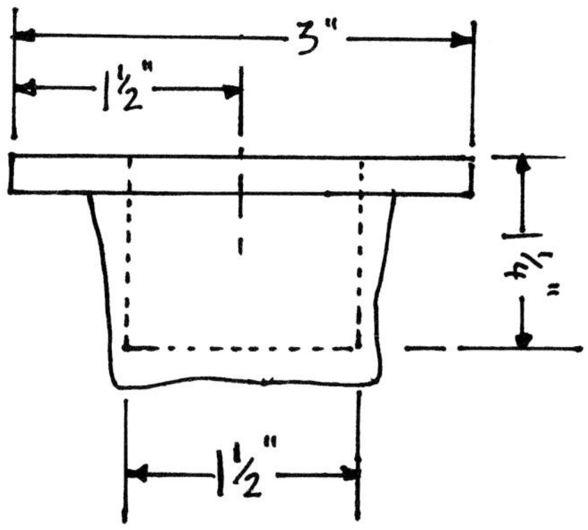

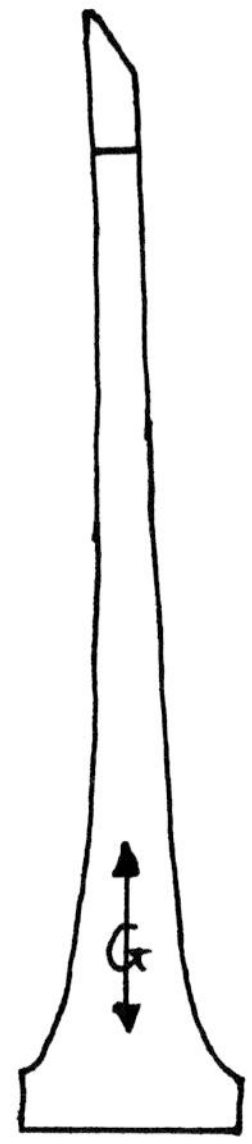

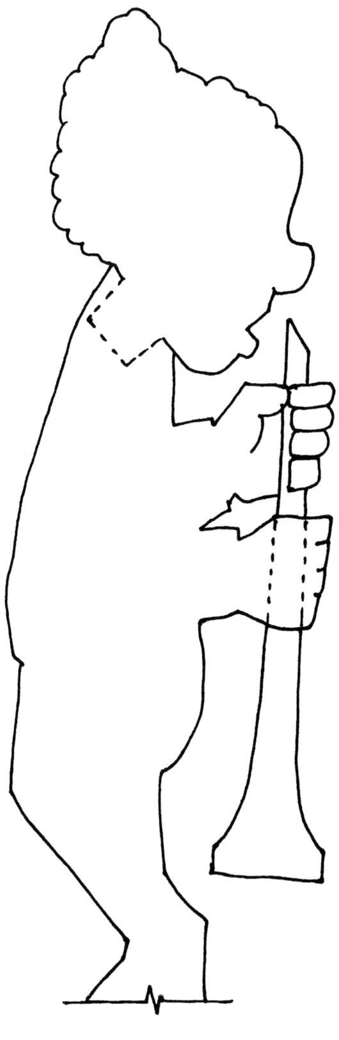

Deacon Lewie

Note: Patterns have been reduced.
Enlarge to 166% for actual size.

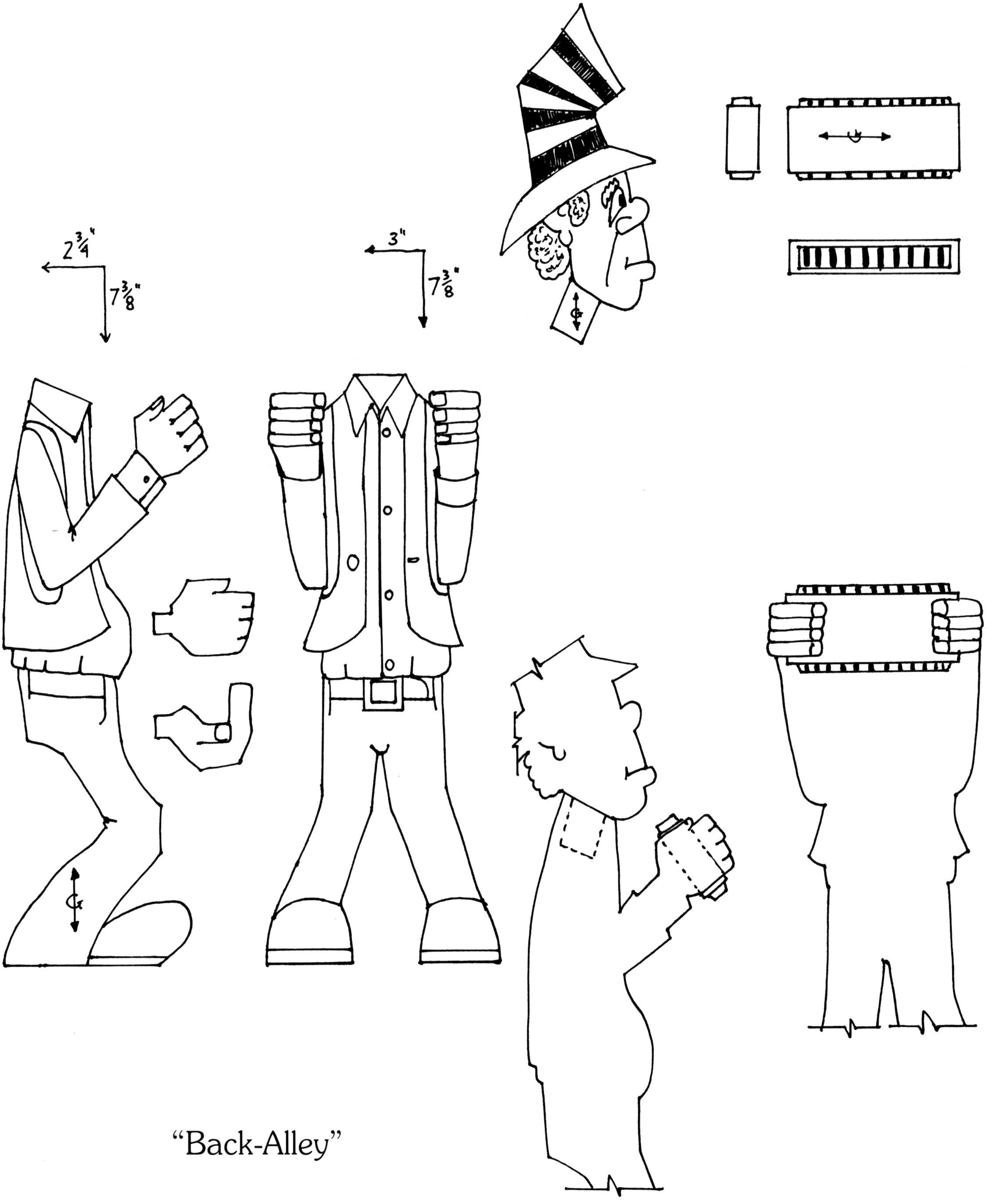

"Back-Alley"

Note: Patterns have been reduced.
Enlarge to 166% for actual size.

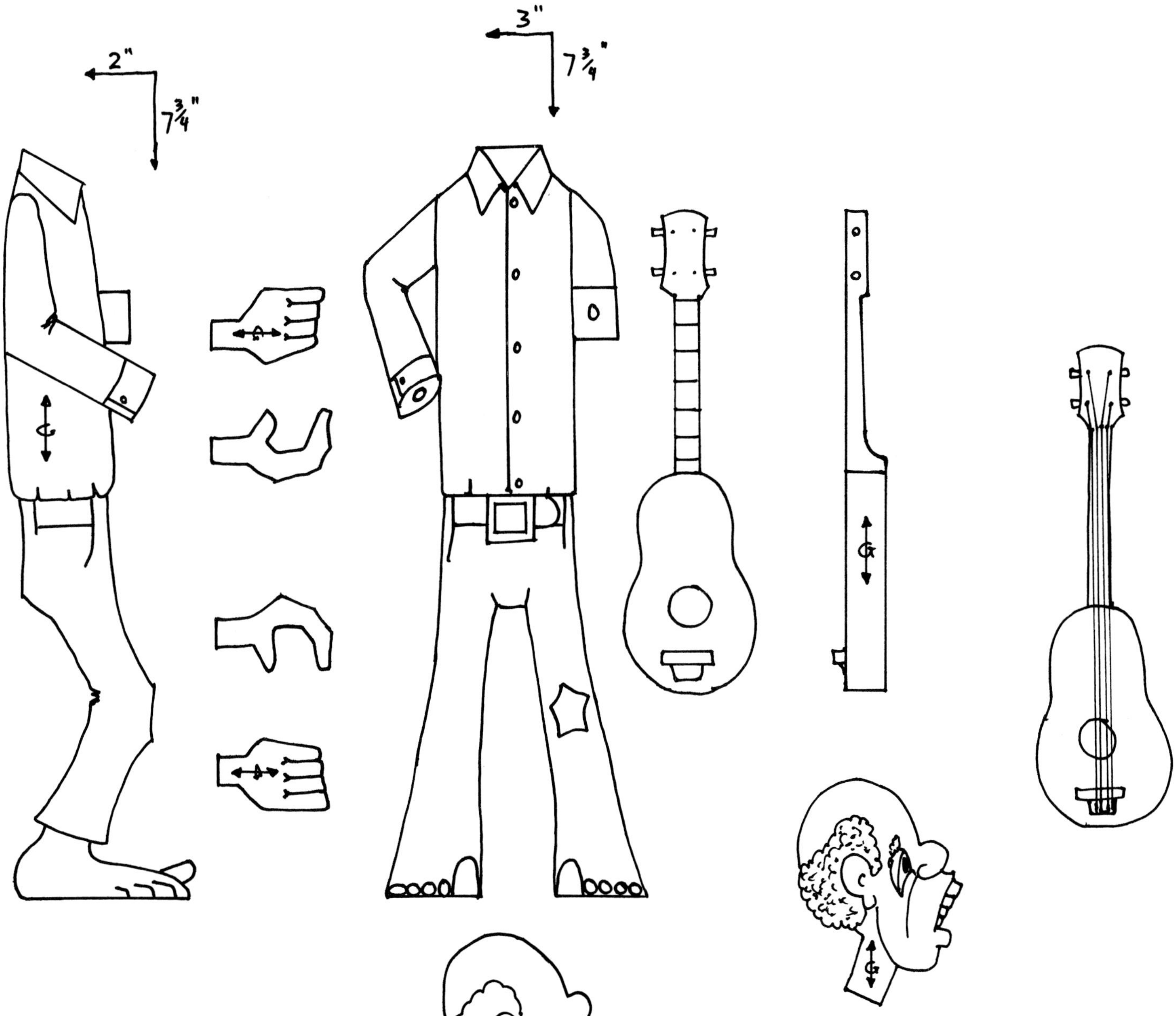

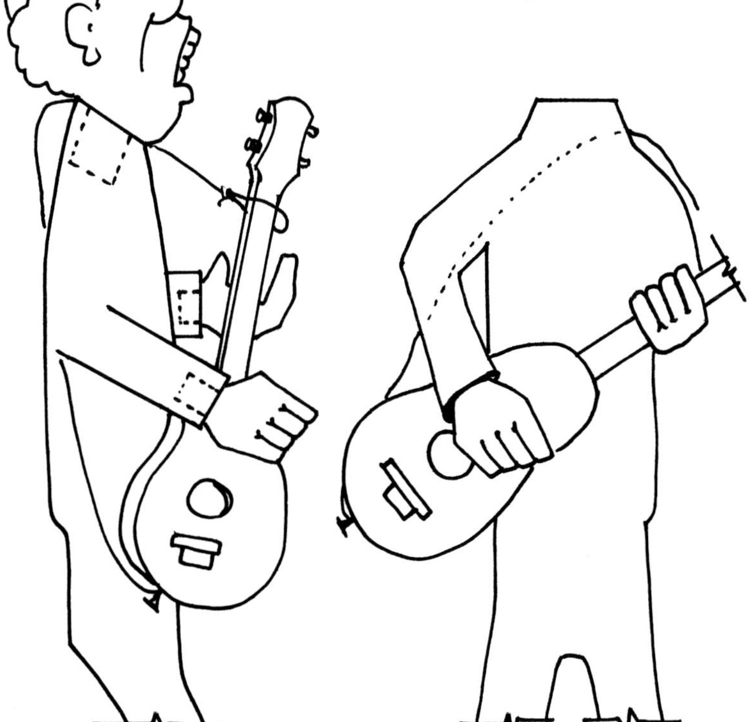

Three-Note Willy

Note: Patterns have been reduced. Enlarge to 166% for actual size.

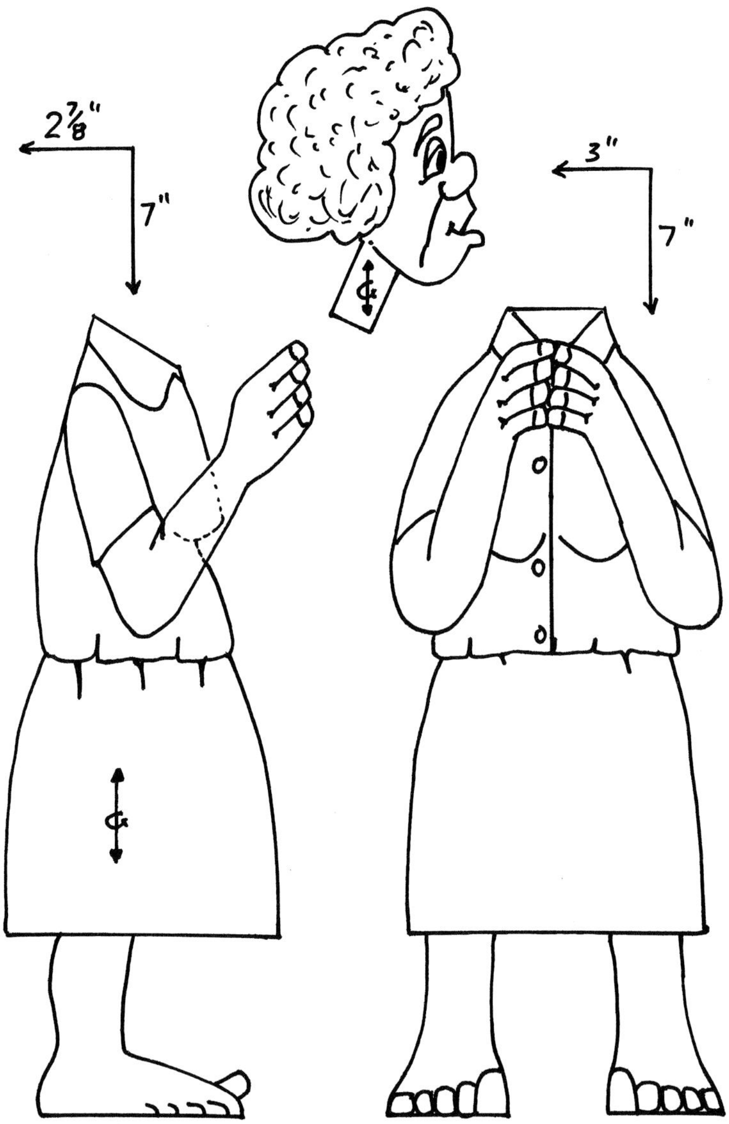

Miss Lucy

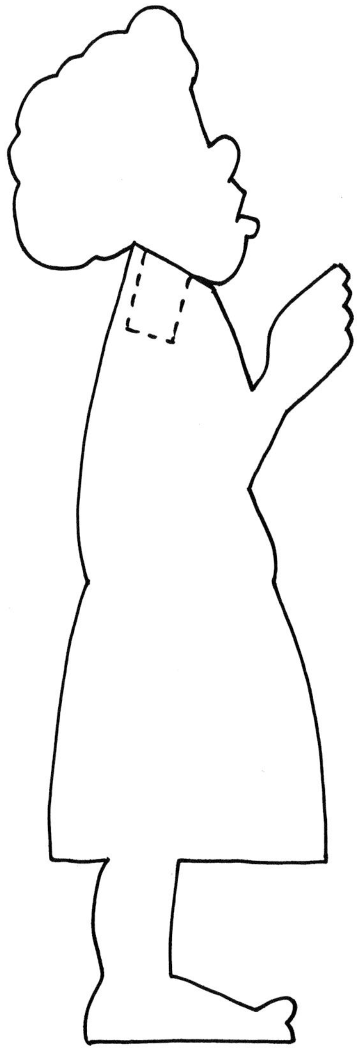

Note: Patterns have been reduced.
Enlarge to 166% for actual size.

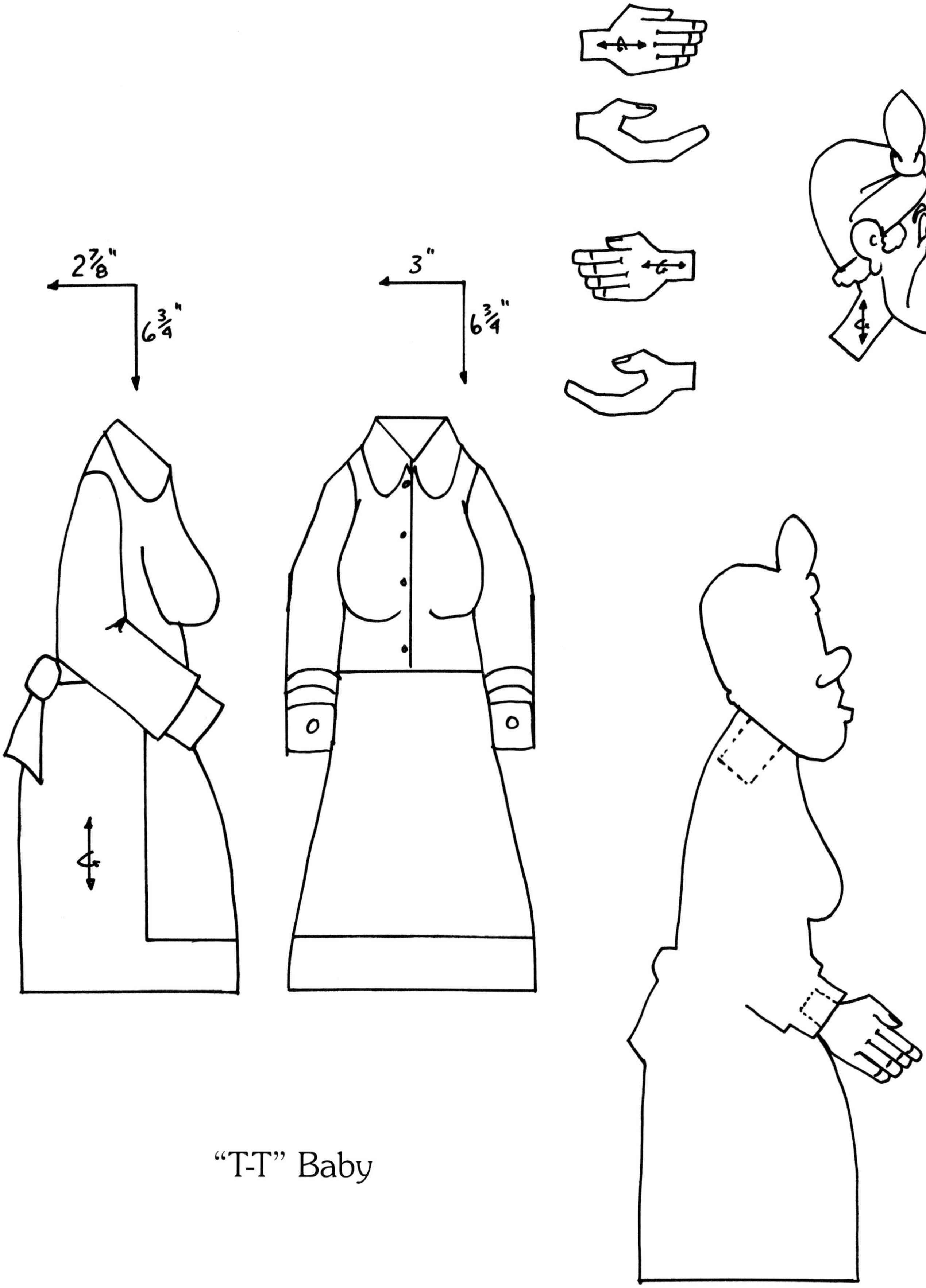

"T-T" Baby

Note: Patterns have been reduced.
Enlarge to 166% for actual size.

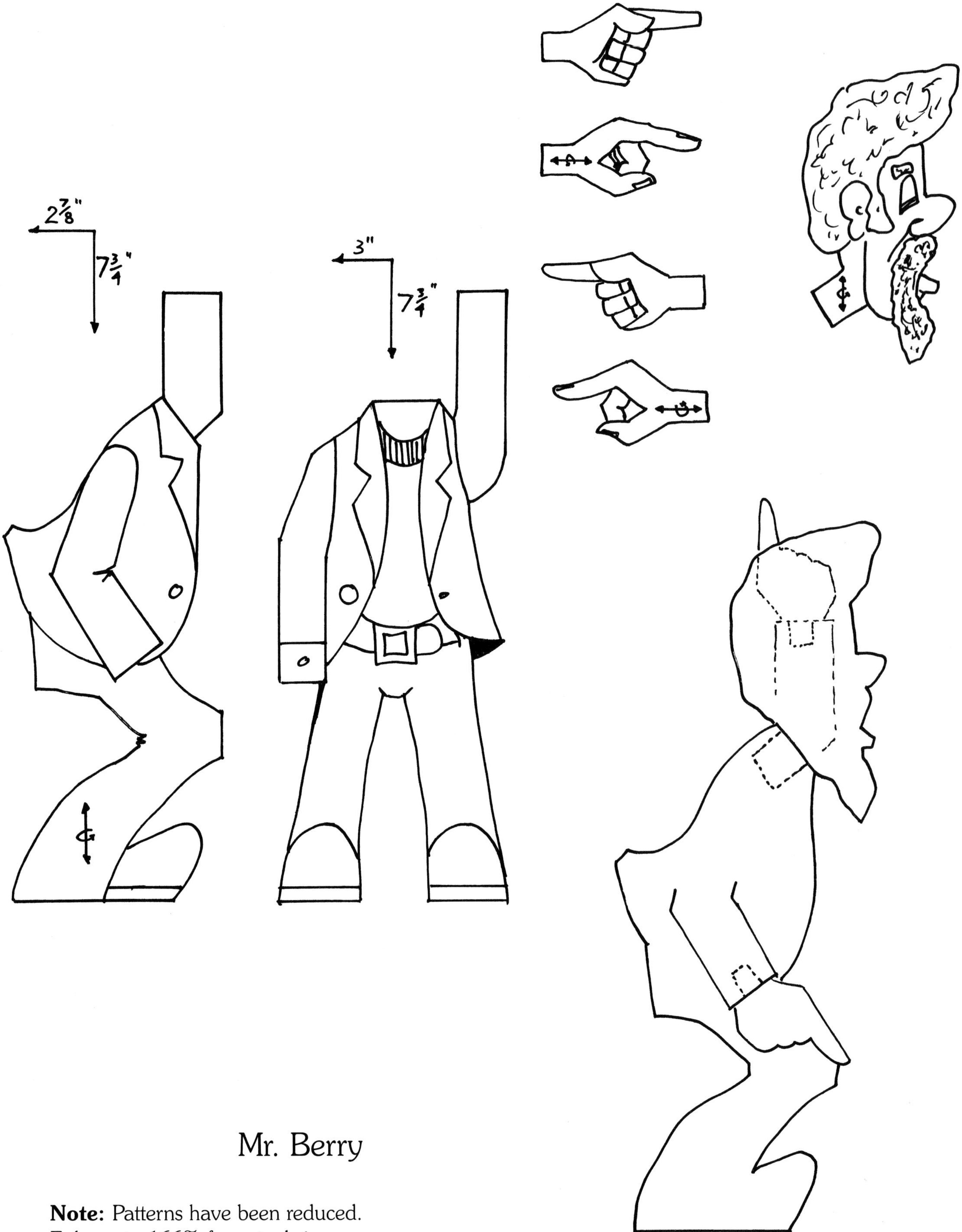

Mr. Berry

Note: Patterns have been reduced.
Enlarge to 166% for actual size.